CREATING OUR COMMON FUTURE

Educating for Unity in Diversity

Edited by

Jack Campbell

Berghahn Books
NEW YORK • OXFORD

WEF Australia

UNESCO Publishing
PARIS

CABRINI COLLEGE LIBRARY
610 KING OF PRUSSIA ROAD
RADNOR, PA 19087

#44764027

Published jointly by
the **United Nations Educational, Scientific and Cultural
Organization**, and **Berghahn Books**

© 2001 UNESCO/WEF

All rights reserved.
No part of this publication may be reproduced in any form or
by any means without the written permission of UNESCO,
and Berghahn Books.

Library of Congress Cataloging-in-Publication Data

Creating our common future : educating for unity in diversity
/ edited by Jack Campbell.
    p.   cm.
Includes bibliographical references.
ISBN 1-57181-279-2 (alk. paper) — ISBN 1-57181-280-6
1. International education. 2. Education—Philosophy.
3. Educational sociology. I. Campbell, W. J. (William John), 1922–

LC1090.C74   2000
370.1—dc21   00-062117

ISBN UNESCO: 92-3-103781-1

British Library Cataloguing in Publication Data

A catalogue record for this book is available from
the British Library.

Printed in the United States on acid-free paper

*The designations employed and the presentation of material throughout this
publication do not imply the expression of any opinion whatsoever on the part of
the UNESCO Secretariat concerning the legal status of any country, territory,
city or area or of its authorities, or the delineation of its frontiers or boundaries.*

*The authors are responsible for the choice and the presentation of the facts
contained in this book and for the opinions expressed therein, which are not
necessarily those of UNESCO and do not commit the Organization.*

The future is not something that happens, but something which is constructed – constructed on our choices, or our failure to choose.... The nature of the major problems which face us show us clearly the nature of those choices. They are not technical but moral choices. They are a statement of what we believe a good society should be.

– Phillip Hughes
Australia 2000: A Shared Challenge, a Shared Response

Remember, if you can imagine it, you can achieve it. If you can dream it, you can become it.

– Peter Njuguna
Delegate to the Youth Forum,
40th International Conference
of World Education Fellowship

CONTENTS

ACKNOWLEDGEMENTS

Grateful acknowledgement is made to the following agencies who during the course of the WEF project supported it with generous financial grants:

Australian Government through its Department of Employment, Education, Training and Youth Affairs – contribution to the 40th International Conference of World Education Fellowship (WEF).

Australian Government through its Department of the Environment and Heritage – contribution to the 40th International Conference of WEF.

Australian Government through its Department of Family Services – contribution to the 40th International Conference of WEF.

Queensland Government through its Ministerial Consultative Council on Curriculum – research grant to enable Stage I to be undertaken.

UNESCO – contribution to the 40th International Conference of WEF; UNESCO contributed, additionally, by meeting the conference expenses of two of its delegates: Professor Colin N. Power and Dr. Rupert McLean.

These sponsors should not be regarded as supporting, by virtue of their grants, any of the views expressed in this book.

Grateful thanks are due, too, to the following members of WEF, who contributed significantly to the book by presenting summary accounts of relevant educational programmes with which they are associated: Dr Stephanie Farrall, Ms Toni Michael and Professor David Woolman, and Ms Helen Cameron. Special thanks are also due to Mr Christopher Strong, AM, President of the Tasmanian Section of WEF, and to his wife, Sally. Their commitment to WEF was demonstrated particularly in the energy that they devoted to raising funds for the 40th International Conference of WEF, and in the spirit of fellowship with which they hosted the Youth Forum. Lastly, the editorial help and professional assistance given by Shawn Kendrick of Berghahn Books are greatly appreciated.

PREFACE

This book reports on a project that was initiated, in consultation with Professor Colin Power, then Deputy Director-General of UNESCO, in order to complement, and contribute to, a series of studies being planned by UNESCO itself (UNESCO 1995, 1996, 1998a, 1998b).

Stage I of the project began with the researchers – Campbell, McMeniman and Baikaloff – collecting open-ended 'vision' statements relating to a desirable society from a sample of 81 Australian people who occupied, or had recently occupied, leadership positions in a variety of organisations. This was followed by the application of a Delphi-type research strategy aimed at determining the measure of consensus within the various visions. (More details are provided in Chapter 3 of this book.)

In Stage II, the project went international when the Australian Council of World Education Fellowship, in association with the International Guiding Committee of WEF, decided to hold a week-long conference in Launceston, Australia, from 29 December 1998 to 4 January 1999, and invited the project director (Campbell) to secure speakers and design a programme that would contribute to the task of converting the visions into reality. This conference, the 40th International Conference of WEF, was attended by nearly three hundred people from all States and Territories of Australia, and from China, France, India, Indonesia, Israel, Japan, Kenya, Korea, New Zealand, the Philippines, South Africa, Sweden, Thailand, the Netherlands, the United Kingdom and the United States.

The publication of this book can be regarded as Stage III of the project. All of its contributors participated at Stage II, and all but two were key participants in Stage I as well. This book is not a proceedings of the conference, but its structure is similar to that of the conference progamme. An introductory chapter is followed by two which focus on normative visions of a common future. Then follow five chapters whose order reflects the findings reported in Chapter 3 – namely, that the creation of a common future, at a *high* level, is dependent upon nurturance of the *human spirit*, and its constituents: *moral responsibility*, and *higher orders of thinking and knowing*, with particular reference to *humane interpersonal relationships* and *sustainability of the environment*. These five chapters include references to educational programmes concerned with the development of these 'transcendent' attributes. The final chapter pulls the threads together.

In its overall conceptualisation, the project takes on board the view that human thinking should contain both imaginative and disciplined elements. In a statement containing allusions drawn from *A Midsummer Night's Dream*, John Passmore (1985: 18) refers to these two elements as 'disciplined imagination' and writes: 'Wherever the disciplined imagination is exercised, there first has to be an envisaging of "the forms of things unknown." ... A teacher must not destroy the child's – or the graduate student's – capacity to fancy. But ultimately that is not enough; the envisaging ... has to be brought to earth, given "a local habitation and a name."' In a similar vein, Garrison (1997: 177) writes:

> ... imagination allows us to unconceal future possibilities in present actualities. When Martin Luther King Jr. declared that he had 'a dream' of a racially harmonious nation, he was not reporting the results of an exercise in pure reason. Reason alone will not provide prophetic moral values, nor was King reporting an empirical fact. Dreams can be perceptions of how things morally *ought* to be, visions of our best possibilities ... Prophetic leaders of all kinds, including visionary teachers, must vividly imagine the ideals and values that they seek to realize through the exercise of practical reasoning. Teachers, too, must be practical reasoners, poets and prophets.

Stage I of the project presented 'visions of our best possibilities' – not the products of unbridled fancy, but statements of what *should* and *could* be – and a full report on this has already been distributed to participants (Campbell, McMeniman and Baikaloff 1992). Stage II was an attempt to bring the envisaging 'to earth' by examining in a disciplined manner how education can contribute to converting the visions to reality. Stage III (this volume) draws upon some of the key findings of the project, with the aim of encouraging all those who are engaged in teaching – whether professionals, parents, youth leaders or others – to lift their sights above the perfectly legitimate but mundane issues of the day, and focus, too, on creating a future of which we can all be proud.

References

Campbell, .J., McMeniman, M.M. and Baikaloff, N. 1992. *Visions of a Future Australian Society: Towards an Educational Curriculum for 2000 AD and Beyond.* Ministerial Consultative Council on Curriculum: Brisbane.

Garrison, J. 1997. *Dewey and Eros: Wisdom and Desire in the Art of Teaching.* Teachers College, Columbia University: New York.

Passmore, J. 1985. Educating for the twenty-first century. *Quadrant* (August).

UNESCO. 1995. *Our Creative Diversity. Report of the World Commission on Culture and Development.* UNESCO Publishing: Paris.

———. 1996. *Learning: The Treasure Within* (Delors Report). Report of the International Commission on Education for the 21st Century. UNESCO Publishing: Paris.

———. 1998a. *World Cultural Report.* UNESCO Publishing: Paris.

———. 1998b. *World Education Report: Teachers and Teaching in a Changing World.* UNESCO Publishing: Paris.

NOTES ON CONTRIBUTORS

Nicholas Baikaloff is a graduate of the University of Queensland (B.Ed.St. and M.Ed. Admin.), specialising in Curriculum. After experience in the TAFE sector of education, he was appointed to the Faculty of Education, Griffith University. He has been on WEF Councils at State and national levels for two decades, including several terms as President of the Queensland Section. He has a particular interest in enhancing links among WEF members nationally and internationally.

Richard J. Bawden is a graduate of the Universities of Queensland (Ph.D.) and London (B.Ag. Sc. Hons). He has recently taken up an appointment as Distinguished Professor, College of Agriculture and Natural Resources, Michigan State University. Prior to that appointment, he was Dean of the Faculty of Agriculture, and, latterly, Director of the Centre for Systemic Development, both at the University of Western Sydney. In January 2000, he was appointed a Member of the Order of Australia for services to agricultural education and rural development.

Elizabeth M. Campbell is a graduate of the Universities of Queensland (Ph.D.), New Zealand (B.A.) and Illinois (A.M.), and holds diplomas of LTCL (piano) and LRSM (singing) from London. Her research interests lie in the field of child development, particularly motivation, and she has lectured in educational psychology at both the Universities of Queensland and Illinois. She has been a member of WEF since 1971, and was editor of the Australian WEF journal, *New Horizons in Education,* from 1990 to 1992.

Jack Campbell is an Emeritus Professor of the University of Queensland, a graduate of the Universities of New Zealand (B.A., M.A. Hons, Senior Scholar) and London (Ph.D.), and has held appointments at the Universities of Otago, Sydney, Kansas, Illinois, Uppsala and Queensland. He has served as President of the Queensland WEF Section, President of the Australian WEF Council (twice) and, since 1994, Hon. Vice-President WEF International.

He is an ANZAAS Mackie Medallist, and in 1994 was appointed an Officer of the Order of Australia.

John Fien, a graduate of the Universities of Queensland (B.A., Ph.D.) and London (M.A.), is the Director of the Griffith University Centre for Innovation and Research in Environmental Education. He has published widely in the fields of environmental education policy and practice in Asia and the Pacific, with a particular focus on action-research networking as a strategy for professional development of teacher educators in the region. His extensive involvement in UNESCO projects includes the Internet-based programme, *Teaching and Learning for a Sustainable Future*.

Brian V. Hill is a graduate of the Universities of Western Australia (B.A., B.Ed. Hons), Sydney (M.A. Hons, University Medal) and Illinois (Ph.D.). He was appointed Foundation Professor and Dean of Education, Murdoch University in 1974, and has held visiting appointments in the UK, NZ, Singapore and the US. His teaching and research interests are in philosophy of education, particularly values education and Christian education, and he has written extensively in a number of fields associated with these interests.

Bruce Keepes is a graduate of the University of Southern California (B.Sc.), Long Beach State University (M.A.) and Stanford University (Ed.D.). He has held appointments at WAIT, the South Australian College of Advanced Education and, most recently, the University of Sydney. His research and teaching interests include learning and computer-based teaching, with a special interest in adaptations for learners with disabilities.

Jillian M. Maling, an Emeritus Professor of the University of Western Sydney, graduated B.A., B.Ed. from the University of Melbourne and Ph.D. from Stanford University. She has served on numerous State and national boards and committees concerned with evaluation and curriculum development, and has published extensively in a number of educational fields. In 1992, she was appointed a Member of the Order of Australia for services to Australian education.

Marilyn M. McMeniman is a graduate of the Universities of Queensland (B.A., Ph.D.) and London (M.A.), and is currently Professor and Dean of the Faculty of Education, Griffith University. Her teaching and research interests include language acquisition and learning, and strategic teaching. She was Foundation Head of the School of Languages and Applied Linguistics at Griffith University during 1994–95. In 1997, she was appointed a Member of the Order of Australia for services to Australian education.

William N. Oats graduated from the Universities of Adelaide (B.A. Hons), Melbourne (B.Ed.) and Tasmania (M.Ed., Ph.D.), and was Australian President of WEF during 1947–48. He had a very distinguished career as a senior teacher at the International School in Geneva and, for 26 years, as Headmaster of The Friends' School, Hobart. In 1970, he was appointed an Officer of the British Empire for services to education and the community. Sadly, Dr Oats died within weeks of completing the chapter in this book.

Colin N. Power is a graduate of the University of Queensland (B.Sc., B.Ed. Hons, Ph.D.) whose most recent appointment was Deputy Director-General of UNESCO. Before taking up the UNESCO appointment in 1989, he was Professor of Education at Flinders University, South Australia, and served as a consultant to ministries of education in South East Asia. He has published widely in the fields of policy studies, science education and assessment, and, in recent years, on issues relating to UNESCO's concerns with providing education for all people, especially those in developing countries.

— One —

INTRODUCTION

e⁀

Jack Campbell

The overarching theme of this book is that if education is to avoid the risk of condemning itself to irrelevance, it must contribute to the resolution of what is seen to be humanity's most pressing challenge – the achievement of unity while retaining, respecting, valuing and encouraging diversity. It is a theme that dominates Chapter 2, in which UNESCO's response to the challenges of creating a global future is surveyed; it is reflected in the Delphi methodology of Chapter 3, which reports on a study concerned with desired futures for Australia; and it appears prominently in each of the five following chapters, which focus, in turn, on the *human spirit, moral responsibility, higher orders of thinking and knowing, humane interpersonal relationships,* and *sustainability of the environment.*

Diversity: An Evolutionary Imperative and the Basis of Species Success

As David Attenborough has reminded us (1979: 293), human beings have been exceptionally successful in establishing themselves and colonising the earth. It has been estimated that ten thousand years ago there were about ten million individuals. Then, four thousand years ago, the number started to increase markedly and, by the first century AD, there were three hundred million. Now, at the beginning of the twenty-first century, the number is around six *billion*. Accompanying this increase in numbers has been a dispersion of humans to all corners of the planet, and in recent years serious thought has been given to establishing habitats in such unlikely places as beneath the sea and beyond Earth.

It has been widely believed that the sudden emergence of *Homo sapiens* as the most numerous of all large animals simply points to the rise of a species which, by a process of natural selection, has become optimally suited to its niche within the cosmos. The problem with this notion, however, is that it implies the *elimination* of genetic diversity, and this has not happened. At conception, each human individual is a unique combination of genes, and varies in tens of thousands of ways from other individuals. Instead of being eliminated, genetic variation has *persisted*. As Tyler (1978: 43), writing in the days before cloning was considered a possibility, explains:

> ... each individual represents a unique selection from an almost infinite number of possible individuals. Large as the earth's population has become ... the number of possible genotypes is infinitely larger, of the order of 70 *trillion*. This is because of the enormous number of genes in the human chromosomes and the much larger number of ways in which they can be combined in sexual reproduction.... Unless a person is a [monozygotic] twin, he or she starts out in life with a genotype different from that of anyone else who has ever lived on earth or will exist in the future.

Within an encompassing *human nature* (comprising such phenomena as innate, developmental programmes and psychological mechanisms), the enormous genetic diversity, to which Tyler refers, is manifested, quantitatively, throughout the genotype's potentialities. These include, *inter alia*, sensory sensitivity, reflexes, perceptual abilities, activity levels, gross motor skills, certain kinds of social behaviour, learning, behavioural plasticity, inventing and acquiring language, higher order conceptualisations, self-awareness and so on, through a long list of (sometimes) highly specific attributes (Buss 1990). In light of what is known about the process of natural selection, the persistence of this seemingly uncoordinated diversity is something of an enigma.

According to Tooby and Cosmides (1990), there are three possible explanations for the persistence of genetic diversity: (a) it is an adaptation, (b) it is a concomitant of an adaptation and (c) it represents random effects. Although these scholars acknowledge that future empirical evidence might establish the possibility of diversity qualifying as an alternative adaptive strategy, they regard this as improbable because of the lack of complexity and 'evidence of special design' (functional coordination) of the variations. In their view, the second of the hypotheses is the most plausible: genetic diversity is a concomitant of an adaptation, namely, sexual reproduction, which has emerged in order to counter the ravages of immense numbers of short-lived, rapidly evolving parasites that quickly adapt to the human host's particular physiology, proteins and biochemistry, and become poised to continue the destruction of all genetically identical individuals. The mixing of genes with those of another individual, in the process of sexual reproduction, creates a completely new genotype, and so the pathogens are denied the headstart of being perfectly adapted to an individual's offspring: '… each new individual constitutes a unique habitat [for pathogens] that must be independently adapted to.' According to this theory, then, genetic diversity is an incidental by-product of an adaptation, not an adaptation *per se*.

In view of the widespread belief that there are major genetic differences among humans based on ethnicity, it is important to note that there are no strong grounds for this position. Gould (1985), Lewontin, Rose and Kamin (1984) and Nei (1987) have all noted that around 85 per cent of human genetic variation is within-group variation, 8 per cent is between tribes or nations within an ethnic group, and only 7 per cent is between ethnic groups. Lewontin, Rose and Kamin (1984: 127) comment: 'The remarkable feature of human evolution and history has been the very small degree of divergence between geographical populations as compared with the genetic variation among individuals.'

Granted that, at conception, human beings are a very diverse population, what happens to them thereafter? One could expect that variability would persist within the phenotype (the observable expression of traits), if only because, in addition to setting trajectories in the initial stages of development, the genotype continues to exert an influence throughout life, for the process of development is one of continuous interaction between an existing matrix and stimuli which arise from within, as well as without, the organism. Despite a number of prenatal influences (humoral communication between the mother and foetus through the placenta,

stimulation from the uterine environment, external stimuli pene-
trating the uterine wall and impinging on the foetus, and stimuli
originating within the foetus itself), in normal circumstances the
new individual is born with most of his or her vast and unique
potential intact. Thereafter, however, the young human begins a
journey through a complex nesting framework of eco-social systems (Bronfenbrenner 1977, 1979, 1989), and whereas some elements from these might enhance variability, most are likely to
have a diminishing effect.

Among the social systems, the family is generally attributed
special potency, and included in its conformity-producing elements is a particular language. While it is not inconceivable that
ancestral conditions which played a part in evolutionary adaptations predispose the young child to acquire the special language
of the parents with particular ease, the weight of evidence is not
supportive of this view. During the 'babbling' stage of development, most if not all of the sounds which feature in human languages make a fleeting appearance, and it is only later that those
of the language in which the youngster is immersed become
dominant, while others subside. The acquisition of a language,
and a particular world-view contained within it, is tantamount to
turning one's back on hundreds of alternative elements of communication as well as cultures.

Other factors which limit the full spectrum of individual variability include exposure to a *common macrosystem* (overarching
institutional patterns of the culture or sub-culture), as well as
common age-graded events (for example, many aspects of the family life cycle, education and occupation), whose nature, timing
and duration occur in highly similar ways for all individuals, and
common history-graded events (for example, economic depressions,
wars, epidemics and social change), which most members of a
given cohort experience. These latter two factors are offset to
some extent by *idiosyncratic personal events*, for example, the
death of a loved one, accidents, disease, divorce, isolated unem-
ployment and the like. (Baltes, Nesselroade and Cornelius 1978;
Baltes, Reese and Lipsett 1980; Baltes and Willis 1979).

Since the young human does not simply 'ingest' elements from
the environment, but rather engages in a complex interaction with
them, the conformity-producing power of these environments is
not as great as might at first be thought. The individual brings to
the interaction not only an established personality matrix with its
own momentum, but also a proneness to filter out disturbing

influences and thereby maintain something like the security of a 'cocoon'. As Hedley Beare states (1991: 3):

> Once born, all of us, both with and without help, begin to spin around ourselves a web of meanings which allow us to interpret our world and also to protect ourselves from its ravages. In the one process, we can ensure our survival, our fulfilment as a creature in the cosmos, and, paradoxically, our imprisonment – enclosed within a world-view and a social fabric which are of our own making and which prevent us from experiencing reality in its wholeness.

Although unique genetic inheritance will always fall far short of complete fulfilment, it and phenotypic variability are still sufficient to ensure that each individual is a living experiment differing from all others. This has great potential survival value but, for maximum capital to be made of it, mechanisms are needed whereby information from the experiments can be accessed. Fortunately, evolution has endowed us with these. First, granted that there are the usual differences in degree, human individuals have both a commitment and an ability to reflect on their own experiences and those of others, and, indeed, to engage in hypothetical thinking about the likely consequences of particular actions. This power of reflection, as Peter Allen states (1990: 565–6), is very important:

> In the biology of simple beings, genetic reproduction ensures that the 'information' about a successful strategy resulting from advantageous genetic variability can only be passed on to descendants. But, of course, an entirely new phase of evolution is reached once information can be 'perceived' and imitative modes of behaviour are possible. The fulcrum of evolution passes from 'genetics' to 'perception-judgment-behaviour'…. Such a mechanism represents a much faster mode of evolution than genetics….

To cap the commitment and ability to reflect, humans have a strong urge and a high ability to communicate. In response to his own question, 'What power did man suddenly acquire that turned him into the most successful of all species?' Attenborough (1979: 308) states, 'The power to communicate', and he goes on to refer to humans as the 'compulsive communicators':

> Man's passion to communicate and to receive communications seems as central to his success as a species as the fin was to the fish or the feather to the birds…. Today, our libraries … can be seen as extra-corporeal DNA, adjuncts to our genetic inheritance as important and

influential in determining the way we behave as the chromosomes in our tissues are in determining the physical shape of our bodies.

The spectacular advances in telecommunications since Attenborough wrote the above have, of course, revolutionised libraries, and have opened up almost unimagined possibilities with respect to the sharing of propositional, practical and experiential knowledge. To some extent, libraries have moved from being collections of materials to facilitators, providing access to material from a wider range of agencies. Those in affluent countries who have the use of modern communications technology can, with a few touches on a keyboard, and in a matter of minutes, gain access to every scholarly paper on a given topic from the leading journals of the world. As Marilyn McMeniman has said (1999: 1): 'We are all hurtling headlong down the cyberspace superhighway – our world is now one of global web-sites, links and networks; a world of digital libraries, teleteaching, teleconferencing and electronic networking – knowledge has become global, international.' The 'Matthew effect', however, is apparent, as colleagues in countries that lack the money to purchase high technology find it more and more difficult to gain access to information (Altbach 1997). As in so many instances, the rich get richer, and the poor get poorer.

The upshot of all this is that when combined with abilities to reflect and communicate, genetic diversity and phenotypic variability ensure that the human species has available an impressive array of knowledge and alternative strategies to assist it in solving adaptation problems. Genetic diversity, which could be said to have initiated the developments, might well, as Tooby and Cosmides claim, have been an 'incidental by-product' of an adaptive strategy, but its importance in evolution is, nevertheless, immense. There could, however, develop a situation in which there is no group cohesion, but simply a collection of individuals, each intent on 'doing his or her own thing'. The challenge is to achieve a measure of unity in diversity, and, for this, it is not sufficient for individuals to be diverse – they need to be *collaborative* as well.

Unity and Collaboration: Social Imperatives

It has often been said that seeing our planet from space as 'a pattern of clouds, oceans, greenery and soils' (World Commission on Environment and Development 1987: 1) was a salutary learning experience for humankind, inasmuch as it destroyed for ever the myths that Earth was the centre of the cosmos, and that humankind was Earth's *raison d'être*. The realisation that human beings, while possessing distinctive characteristics, are at one with the environment, however, is neither new nor revolutionary. It was the *Weltanschauung* of the pre-Christian Greco-Roman world, and features prominently in the Buddhist teaching that is called *Esho Funi*, the indivisible unity of total environment and total greater life force. It also features prominently in many indigenous cultures around the world. Thus, prior to the arrival of the Europeans, the world-view held by Australian Aborigines was one in which humans were an integral part of nature, sharing with other species the same life essence.

Within our global ecosystem, human beings are presently *sine qua non* – only they can ensure that the 'health' of the total system is maintained at a sustainable or optimum level. If they act against the interests of the system, Earth might not survive, although Lovelock (1988: 236) makes the interesting suggestion that Earth (Gaia) will survive, but humans will not: 'Any species (that is, any part of Gaia) that adversely affects the environment is doomed; but life goes on.... Gaia is not purposefully antihuman, but so long as we continue to change the global environment against her preferences, we encourage our replacement with a more environmentally seemly species.' Shades of Paul Davies' notion (1990) of an overall design in which humans play a key role.

Within the ideational context of humans needing to collaborate with all living and non-living elements on the planet, the emphasis in this book is on encouraging them to collaborate with one another. The assumption is that it is the *collaborative* individual who will contribute most to both his or her own welfare and that of the species. Individualism and common good are not seen to be in competition; rather, the former is intimately interlocked with the latter and, moreover, culminates in it. As Sir Percy Nunn wrote eight decades ago (1920), 'Individuals are never more themselves, never more masters of their own fate, than when they recognise that they are part of a greater whole, from which they can draw inspiration and strength, and to which they can give inspiration and strength.'

Granted that it may be in the 'natural order of things' for humans to collaborate, it is easy to be fooled by present events. As Edward de Bono has said (1990: 38), 'If we look at the area of human affairs we see poverty, wars, racism, prejudice, ecological disasters, violence, crime, terrorism, greed, selfishness and short-term thinking.' This century may well have been the nadir in the history of human relationships. The Holocaust, two world wars, the slaughter of millions of innocent women and children in a series of ongoing, 'ethnic-cleansing' acts, the exhortation 'To kill, to kill and to kill', often in the name of one's own god – all of these, and other, brutal, self-inflicted 'crimes against humanity' must have, at times, left those gods wondering if the human species would, or should, survive into the twenty-first century.

The depressing picture presented above suggests an urgent need for a paradigmatic shift in human relationships. And there are other factors which suggest this, too. Prominent among these is the accelerating movement towards globalisation, which is reflected in a number of trends: migration of persons across State boundaries, resulting in ethnic clashes of culture and competing claims, as in Kosovo in recent times; 'hybridisation', as a result of the relentless flow of information, media symbols and images, and political and cultural ideas; threats to the common global environment as a result of overpopulation, poverty, inappropriate use of resources, extension of Western consumption patterns, climatic change, ozone depletion, desertification and the like; the interdependent working of political economies; the capacity of military weapons to make a mockery of State boundaries; and the emergence of a 'common ethic', accompanied by an unwillingness on the part of organisations such as the United Nations and NATO to stand by while 'domestic' atrocities flourish in many quarters of the globe.

In a paper which draws upon her experiences as a participant in the Oslo negotiations between the PLO and the Israeli government, Marianne Heiberg (1995) endorses Einstein's view that 'The thinking which has brought us to this stage cannot carry us beyond it'. Her thesis is that the concept of territorial sovereignty, which has served small and weak States well in the past, is now 'a formula for endless conflict in a modern world marked by interdependence and intricate ethnic diversity'. She believes that the solution for the Middle East/North Africa region lies in following the example of the European community:

> In Europe, sovereignty is being tamed and transformed by a process of trans-national community building, linking local communities into broader associations, breaking the monopoly of the territorial state, making the latter less all-encompassing and less sovereign, creating

multiple identities also across borders, transforming relations between citizens and societies, societies and states. Keeping the peace
depends to a considerable degree on the creation of non-territorial
cultural and functional sovereignties within the context of a European community.

In support of this position, it can be noted that some of the most
striking examples of international collaboration, such as space
and Antarctic research, are occurring where territorial sovereignty is minimally involved.

Paige Porter (1997: 94–5) presents some of the challenges
which face us:

> In a complex mass society, we need to come to terms, at one and the
> same time, with how we can strive for equality, how we can respect
> difference, and how we can develop new understandings of our *social*
> condition. Some of the questions are: what do we have in common,
> what do we need to share, what do we need to be jointly responsible
> for, and what processes best enable us to achieve these understand-
> ings? How can social cohesion be furthered when there is a height-
> ened awareness of difference? How can an active civic culture with
> strong public civic discourse be developed and maintained in a more
> fragmented society?

Role and Concept of Education

It is widely accepted that education is a crucial agency in developing a sustainable measure of unity in diversity. As the Delors
Report states (UNESCO 1996):

> In confronting the many challenges that the future holds in store,
> humankind sees in education an indispensable asset in its attempt to
> attain the ideals of peace, freedom and justice. As it concludes its
> work, the Commission affirms its belief that education has a funda-
> mental role to play in personal and social development. The Com-
> mission does not see education as a miracle cure or a magic formula
> opening the door to a world in which all ideals will be attained, but as
> one of the principal means available to foster a deeper and more har-
> monious form of human development and thereby to reduce poverty,
> exclusion, ignorance, oppression and war.

But two caveats should be made. First, as implied in the
UNESCO statement above, the function of education is not that

of direct problem-solving but of nurturing within individuals those characteristics of thinking and feeling which will enable them to contribute significantly, along with others, to creating the best possible global future. Second, education needs to be conceived as being broader than *formal schooling* (the education which is delivered by means of an institutionalised system, chronologically graded from pre-school, through primary and secondary, to various forms of post-secondary). It needs to include, as well, *non-formal* educational experiences (i.e. those out-of-school activities which are organised by many different public and private agencies) and *informal* ones (i.e. the host of day-to-day interactions in which we all engage and which, by touching us, educate us). For millions of people (perhaps as many as a billion) throughout the world, informal education is all that they will ever receive; for others, this mode will be supplemented by non-formal programmes aimed at eradicating illiteracy or providing basic opportunities to develop work skills. Initially, these latter programmes were directed at adults, but especially since the World Conference on Education for All (1990) in Jomtien, Thailand, there has been an extension (notably in Thailand, Indonesia and India) aimed at reaching the 135 million children aged 6–14 who do not have access to the formal school system (Power 1992: 28). Considered globally, however, the majority of humans receive their education through all three modes: *informal* is inescapable; *non-formal* is becoming more and more frequent, not only in the developing countries but in developed ones, too, as re-training and lifelong learning become accepted features; *formal* is common, at least to primary level, in most parts of the world.

Arising out of the research by Coleman *et al.* (1966), Jencks *et al.* (1972), and Heath and Nielson (1974), it has sometimes been argued that home background (which, it should be said, includes healthy components of all three modes of education) explains almost all of the variance in student learning outcomes, leaving virtually nothing that can be attributed to schooling. The replacement of these large survey studies by more sophisticated case-study ones, however, reveals overwhelming evidence to support the conventional view that formal schooling can make a great difference (Ceci 1991; Husen and Tuijnman 1991). Moreover, even if the *average* effect of formal education were small – and it is not – the effect upon particular groups (such as the disadvantaged) has always been immense. We probably all know of people whose life opportunities have been greatly enhanced as a result of school experiences. At the time of this writing, a Queensland State funeral is being held for Neville Bonner, the first Aborigine to enter an Australian parliament. Bonner was raised in the most impoverished of environments, did not attend any formal school until his teens and then progressed only as far as Year 3. Nevertheless, his few years of schooling enabled him to become sufficiently competent in literacy for him to take control of his own learning, and he went on to become a truly great Australian who made a major contribution to reconciling deep-rooted racial disharmony within our society.

Formal education need not, of course, denote one adult teaching 30 or so children within a traditional classroom. As Marilyn McMeniman said recently (1999: 1): 'We now have schools, universities, businesses and services without walls, that are continuously accessible via interactive television, that are global and that can be accessed without leaving one's home.' Sue Graham and Pauline Donaldson (1997) provide a good illustration of this when they tell of their experiences as LEARNZ teachers in the 'global laboratory' of Antarctica, where they served as links between researchers stationed at Cape Roberts and students and teachers back in New Zealand. Among their main means of communication, in addition to videos, was the LEARNZ web site, which was regularly updated with digital pictures, transcripts of audioconferences, a daily diary from Antarctica, technical advice, links to other Antarctic sites, reports of research relating to the health of the planet and the role of humans in causing change, and the like. As these teachers comment, 'Talking with a teacher who has just spent the night sleeping in a snow mound at minus 30 degrees close to Mt Erebus, or slept in a polar tent perched above the Southern Ocean on two metres of sea ice, and asking questions of your teacher actually in a penguin colony, certainly adds excitement to the business of learning.'

That informal education, too, can be highly effective is illustrated in this delightful passage from Richard Bawden (1991: 30), in which he reports on how his three young children set about achieving their own small world of unity in diversity by bridging the language and culture gaps between Australia and Uruguay:

> On January 4 1975, I watched as my three little children learned how to learn to speak Spanish. Rushing into the garden of our new abode in Montevideo, they called out to the little girl next door, 'Hello'. 'Ola' she

responded. 'Ola' the Bawden triad then chorused, mimicking not just the sound, but the flamboyant gesture that went with it! From my own state of linguistic paralysis, I marvelled over the ensuing weeks as they learned how to converse by constructing whole new sentences in their new language. As they came to know Spanish, so they came to do Spanish-type things which was consistent with becoming part of their new Uruguayan culture. Through language they were learning to know, to do, and to be ... all at the same time; indeed each way of knowing was vital for the other two, and they seemed somehow to know that too!

At four, five and seven years of age, my young children had themselves taken control of the management of the way they were transforming their novel experiences into knowledge as the vehicle for adaptation to their new environment.

Perhaps the safest conclusion is that while all three modes *can* be highly effective, much will depend on slightly less inclusive characteristics – such as priority of goals, educational objectives, physical contexts, psychological climates, curricula, teaching styles, and assessment and reporting – within each. This issue will be returned to in several of the later chapters.

References

Allen, P. 1990. Why the future is not what it was. *Futures*, vol. 22, no. 6, 555–70.

Altbach, P.G. 1997. Information, power and education. *Australian Educational Researcher*, vol. 24, no. 1.

Attenborough, D. 1979. *Life on Earth*. Collins: BBC.

Baltes, P.B., Nesselroade, J.R. and Cornelius, S.W. 1978. Multivariate antecedents of structural change in development: a simulation of cumulative environmental patterns. *Multivariate Behavioural Research*, vol. 13, 127–52.

Baltes, P.B., Reese, H.W. and Lipsett, L.P. 1980. Life-span developmental psychology. *Annual Review of Psychology*, 65–110.

Baltes, P.B., and Willis, S.L. 1979. Life-span developmental psychology, cognition and social policy. In M.W. Riley (ed.). *Aging from Birth to Death*. Westview: Boulder.

Bawden, R. 1991. Whose learning is it anyway? A justification of learner-managed learning. *New Horizons in Education*, vol. 85.

Beare, H. 1991. The womb and the cocoon: some observations on parenting and schooling. *New Horizons in Education*, vol. 85.

Bronfenbrenner, U. 1977. Towards an experimental ecology of human development. *American Psychologist*, vol. 32, 513–31.
———. 1979. *The Ecology of Human Development*. Harvard University Press: Cambridge, MA.
———. 1989. Ecological systems theory. In R. Vasta (ed.). *Annals of Child Development*, vol. 6. JAI Press: Greenwich, Conn.
Buss, D.M. 1990. Toward a biologically informed psychology of personality. *Journal of Personality*, vol. 58, no. 1.
Ceci, S.J. 1991. How much does schooling influence general intelligence and its cognitive components? A reassessment of the evidence. *Developmental Psychology*, 27.
Coleman, J.S., *et al*. 1966. *Equality of Educational Opportunity*. Office of Education, US Dept. of Health, Education and Welfare: Washington, DC.
Davies, P. 1990. *God and the New Physics*. Penguin: London.
de Bono, E. 1990. *I Am Right – You Are Wrong*. Viking: London.
Gould, S.J. 1985. Human equality is a contingent fact of history. In *The Flamingo's Smile: Reflections in Natural History*. Norton: New York.
Graham, S., and Donaldson, P. 1997. Putting the curriculum on ice. *Computers in New Zealand Schools*, vol. 9, no. 2.
Heath, R.W., and Nielson, M.A. 1974. The research basis for performance-based teacher education. *Review of Educational Research*, vol. 44.
Heiberg, M. 1995. Building Cohesion in the Wake of the Israeli-Palestinian Conflict: The Question of Sovereignty. Paper delivered, Sydney.
Husen, T., and Tuijnman, A. 1991. The contribution of formal schooling to the increase in educational capital. *Educational Researcher*, vol. 20.
Jencks, C., *et al*. 1972. *Inequality: A Reassessment of the Effects of Family and Schooling in America*. Basic Books: New York.
Lewontin, R.C., Rose, S. and Kamin, L.J. 1984. *Not in Our Genes: Biology, Ideology and Human Nature*. Pantheon: New York.
Lovelock, J. 1988. *Gaia: A New Look at Life on Earth*. Oxford University Press: London.
McMeniman, M.M. 1999. Engaging the Educational Vision: Handing Control to the Imaginative and Empathic Learner. Paper presented at the 40th International Conference of WEF, Launceston.
Nei, M. 1987. *Molecular Evolutionary Genetics*. Columbia University Press: New York.
Nunn, P. 1920. *Education: Its Data and First Principles*. Arnold and Co.: London.
Porter, P. 1997. Knowledge, skills and compassion. *Australian Educational Researcher*, vol. 24, no. 1.
Power, C.N. 1992. Education for all: a developing-country perspective with particular reference to non-formal approaches. *New Horizons in Education*, vol. 86.

Tooby, J. and Cosmides, L. 1990. On the universality of human nature and the uniqueness of the individual: the role of genetics and adaptation. *Journal of Personality*, vol. 58, no. 1.

Tyler, L.E. 1978. *Individuality*. Jossey-Bass: San Francisco.

UNESCO. 1996. *Learning: The Treasure Within* (Delors Report). Report of the International Commission on Education for the 21st Century. UNESCO Publishing: Paris.

World Commission on Environment and Development. 1987. *Our Common Future*. Oxford University Press: London.

World Conference on Education for All. 1990. *World Declaration on Education for All*. Interagencies Commission: Jomtien, Thailand.

Two

UNESCO's Response to the Challenge of Establishing Unity in Diversity

Colin N. Power

Introduction

The World Education Fellowship (WEF) and UNESCO were both created in the aftermath of world wars, and they share a common vision and a common mission. WEF was established soon after the First World War and brought together people from diverse fields (not just educators) and from many countries who were determined to create a better world through education, a world in which the dignity of all people would be respected. Conceived while the bombs were still falling in the darkest hours of the Second World War, UNESCO was the outcome of the reflections of Allied leaders who, mindful of the failures and misuses of education in totalitarian regimes, were determined to ensure that education would be re-designed so as to build a better future for all. The founders of UNESCO were men and women with a vision which has become enshrined in its Constitution: 'Since wars begin in the minds of men, it is in the minds of men that the defences of peace must be constructed.' But not peace at any price: peace founded on respect for the dignity and basic rights of all, and on 'the intellectual and moral solidarity of mankind'.

I have begun by stressing that global organisations like WEF and UNESCO have a common vision and a mission which unite them. I will also argue that this common vision, and the values which inspire it, are widely shared across many cultures, and have withstood the test of time. While stressing the unity of purpose and vision, I acknowledge that there are important differences from one culture to another in the meanings and priorities assigned to the values that are gaining universal consensus. Understanding culturally embedded nuances in these meanings and priorities is vitally important whenever we seek to translate a shared vision to action in a given cultural and temporal setting.

In our constantly changing global village, the rapidity and scope of the transformations underway not only link our fate increasingly with that of others but also, somewhat paradoxically, create greater political and economic uncertainty, larger gaps between nations and greater cultural diversity within them. In an intensely competitive but shared world, we must discover ways by which diverse cultural groups can live together, respect the dignity and worth of each person and culture, and learn to share and care about our common future. Unity in diversity is difficult, but it is the only option. As UNESCO's Report of the World Commission on Culture and Development (UNESCO 1995b) suggests: '... co-operation between people ... from different cultures will be facilitated and conflict kept within acceptable and even constructive limits, if participants see themselves as being bound and motivated by shared commitments. It is, therefore, imperative to look for a core of shared ethical values and principles.'

Beyond the intercultural challenges which globalisation has brought, there has come a significant, often negative, impact on the social institutions (family, community, school, church or mosque) that form the context within which our children develop. In particular, many countries are deeply worried about the problem of drugs, AIDS, corruption and violence – seeing them as manifestations of an underlying 'moral crisis' or 'ethical vacuum'. Indeed, the most serious threats to peace and security are now *within* our nations, rather than between them. Community concerns in all regions of the world are leading to calls to produce a statement of values, a code of morals to guide educational policy and practice.

UNESCO's Search for Common Values

We live in a world in which some ten thousand societies, each with several cultures, co-exist in about two hundred States.

Building peace and resolving conflicts globally, or within any society, is not possible unless there is an underlying unity in the diversity of cultures and religions. Much of the work of UNESCO has involved the quest for that unity, for a universal set of values and minimal standards which all societies and recognised religions will accept. The Report of the World Commission on Culture and Development (UNESCO 1995b) defines these underlying common values as 'a global ethics' and sees the principles of democracy, peace, human rights and pluralism as basic ingredients. But, at the same time, our global ethic stresses respect for the dignity and worth of every individual, every culture. How does one combine the universality of core values with an acknowledgement of different cultures, social interests and individual freedoms? Seeking an answer to this question is prominent on the agenda of UNESCO. Our vision and action must combine universalistic principles with cultural differences, and our debate must include and respect everybody – every cultural and social group, particularly those who are currently excluded. As Touraine (UNESCO 1998a) stresses:

> The idea which must never be sacrificed is that peace within each society and between societies cannot exist without the recognition, first and foremost, of a universalist principle which prevails over both the instrumental reason which rules the economy and cultural diversity.… Education must not be merely a means of strengthening society: it must also serve to build personalities capable of innovating, resisting and communicating, affirming their universal right, and acknowledging that of others, to participate in the modern technical age with their own personalities, memories, languages and desires.

UNESCO has continued the process of dialogue among the religions, philosophies, cultures and educators of the world in the search for a common sub-stratum of values that make co-existence possible on a worldwide scale, and that provide a global dimension to the curriculum and to our rights and responsibilities as citizens of a given nation and of the world. The dialogues conducted as part of the UNESCO Universal Ethics Project (UNESCO 1998c) are revealing 'reflectively and methodologically' that there are several key values and principles that are valid across cultures, religions and societies, and that will help humanity deal with global problems in the immediate future. The methodological approach begins with an empirical search for values and principles that are widely held and factually recognised in a diversity of cultures and religions. Theoretically, reflectively, this work shows the centrality of values relating to human rights as articulated in UNESCO's Universal Declaration of Human Rights (UNESCO 1948). The concept of human rights as currently formulated in the Universal Declaration is a comparatively recent invention. Though just 50 years old, its origins stem from historical struggles for freedom, equality and justice, and its formulation has been strongly influenced by the declarations of the American Revolution and the French Revolution. Empirically, based on public opinion surveys in many countries of the world, there is wide agreement that concern for others, responsibility, good manners, tolerance and respect for other people are important values to promote.

Common Values and Education

The Universal Declaration of Human Rights, referred to above, includes Article 26, within which there are three key elements focusing on education:

1. Everyone has the right to education. Education shall be free, at least in the elementary and fundamental stages. Elementary education shall be compulsory. Technical and professional education shall be made generally available and higher education shall be equally available on the basis of merit.
2. Education shall be directed to the full development of the human personality and to the strengthening of respect for human rights and fundamental freedoms. It shall promote understanding, tolerance and friendship among all nations, racial and religious groups, and shall further the activities of the United Nations for the maintenance of peace.
3. Parents have a right to choose the kind of education that shall be given to their children.

Element 1 of Article 26 is a necessary, but not a sufficient, condition for democracy, peace and tolerance. Element 2 reminds us of the why and what: education must be 'directed to the full development of the human personality and to the strengthening of respect for human rights and fundamental freedoms', and Element 3 reminds us of the centrality of the family (and implicitly of its cultures and values), rather than the State, in choosing the kind of education needed. In the fifty years that have passed since the Universal Declaration was proclaimed, almost all countries have ratified it and are thus legally bound by its articles. A surprisingly large number of national educational laws contain the key elements of Article 26.

Basic education for all is an essential condition for participatory democracy, and nations around the world have repeatedly re-affirmed the principle of free, compulsory primary education for everyone, without exception, and with some recent success. Within developing countries, however, the 1980s were a decade of lost opportunities and thwarted aspirations for education. Scarcely noticed by the media and the world public, basic education for children and their parents in the poorer countries suffered stagnation and decline. Entire school systems stopped growing. In every fifth developing country, primary student numbers fell irrespective of rapid population growth.

The response of UNESCO to this challenge was to convene the World Conference on Education for All in Jomtien, Thailand, in March 1990. As a result of this initiative, a global commitment to provide education for all was re-formulated, and Declaration and Action Frameworks were adopted at the national, regional and international levels. UNESCO has continued to organise follow-up conferences; mobilise support from such organisations as UNDP, UNICEF and the World Bank; establish global and national networks; and serve as a clearing-house for the exchange of information. Without this initiative, stimulation and facilitation by UNESCO, the provision of basic education in parts of Africa, Asia, the Pacific, Latin America and the Caribbean might well have continued to decline, whereas the years since 1990 have witnessed a steady movement towards the goals endorsed at Jomtien. This welcome turn around was revealed six years later in the Education for All Forum in Amman, Jordan (UNESCO 1996b).

A recent UNESCO document, *Towards a Culture of Peace* (UNESCO 1997), submitted to the 1997 General Assembly of the UN, outlines the extent to which there is an agreed ethical basis, a set of universal principles for developing and assessing educational programmes for a desirable future society, both global and national. The document makes it clear that, from an international perspective, the basic human values on which education should be built are those which have been established and reaffirmed over the years in a number of standard-setting instruments, beginning with the Constitutions of the UN and UNESCO and the Universal Declaration of Human Rights, and more recently in the *Declaration and Integrated Framework for Action on Education for Peace, Human Rights and Democracy* (UNESCO 1995a). The challenge is to ensure that these values – which centre on human rights and the dignity and worth of each individual and culture, rather than those which are based on a given economic ideology or imposed by any powerful political, religious or cultural group – help to define educational priorities and practices. For too long, we have defined development and legitimated national policies on the basis of short-sighted economic and political models which serve the immediate interests of powerful countries and their elites. As the 1995 World Summit for Social Development confirmed, the values and assumptions of the market model are badly flawed. The type of development they promote is neither equitable nor sustainable.

In agreeing to aim at both global unity and individual and cultural diversity, educationists have taken on a much harder task than formerly attempted. In the past, in those few countries in which there was only one official religion, the church, temple or mosque provided the necessary authority to impose a common moral code on schools. For the others, in which there were a number of potentially conflicting religions and cultures, harmony and some measure of national unity were achieved through the establishment of secular public education systems. Unity assumed precedence over respecting the diversity of cultures, human rights and fundamental freedoms. In countries like Australia, Britain, France and the US, the school served as a melting pot wherein migrant and indigenous cultures were subsumed by the dominant culture's language and religious values. In Australia, for example, education was too often used as a tool of assimilation and played a key role in the loss of cultural identity for all those of non-Celtic origins. Two hundred years ago there were approximately 260 different Aboriginal languages in use, and estimates put dialectal variation at between 500 and 600, but today only about 100 are spoken by at most even a handful of people, and only about 25 are being passed on to children (Fesl 1987). The Australian scenario is repeated worldwide. According to Davis (1999: 65), 'Throughout all of history something of the order of 10,000 spoken languages have existed. Today, of the roughly 6,000 languages still spoken, many are not being taught to children – effectively they are already dead – and only 300 are spoken by more than a million people.' The priceless diversity of human language and the modes of thinking and classification which go with it, and which have evolved over tens of thousands of years in the cultures of our indigenous peoples, have been lost for ever.

The melting pot model meant that the literature, history, languages, traditions and norms which Australian children learned at school emphasised the country's British heritage. They learned almost nothing of the values and ways of life of indigenous Australian peoples or of their Asia-Pacific neighbours. But the melting pot analogy is no longer acceptable. Slowly it is being realised that the recognition of individual and cultural diversity is required by democratic principles of equity, human rights and self-determination. Slowly, too, cultural diversity is being seen as an asset, rather than a liability, in as far as, like biological diversity, it provides the basic elements for adaptation and survival in times of change or crisis. We need to replace the melting pot model by a mosaic, rich in diversity but, nonetheless, having a clear, unifying pattern based on 'global ethics'. Can this be achieved? Long ago, one of my heroes, Mahatma Gandhi, gave us an answer: 'I do not want my house to be walled in on all sides and my windows to be stuffed. I want the culture of all lands to be blown about my house as freely as possible. But I refuse to be blown off my feet by any.' Gandhi remains an inspiration to all those who seek to oppose violence and to mobilise diverse groups in support of a larger vision of unity. He understood the value of cultural diversity.

The challenge is great and the stakes are high. We are living in a world characterised by inequity, poverty, violence, drug abuse and exclusion, as well as new threats to security and social cohesion stemming from the economic and social structural transformations of the information age. Globalisation and new communication technologies threaten further marginalisation of the poor and minority cultures. We are witnessing a rise everywhere of intolerance, violence, ultranationalism and xenophobia – the fear of difference of any kind, whether skin colour, language, ethnic origin or sex. Frequently, these conflicts and tensions draw on the many sources of individual and community frustration created by the spread of poverty, exclusion and injustice. We are being repeatedly warned, too, of the crisis facing the earth's fragile ecosystems, of the dangers inherent in squandering our planet's riches and of the threats to the collective future posed by population growth, deforestation and pollution, which are exterminating roughly one plant or animal species every thirty minutes. The Rio Conference (UNICED 1992) tried to stem the destruction, but in an intensely competitive world, few nations have been willing to take the steps which most people acknowledge are fundamental to our common future. Two timid conventions were signed, the words 'sustainable development' and 'Agenda 21' were brandished about, but little happened.

Frameworks for Debate and Action

I would now like to move a little along the road from visions to action by outlining some possible frameworks for future education which derive from universally accepted values and a recognition of the richness and diversity of cultures.

To begin with, I would like to propose that we think of an education programme which aims at promoting multiple citizenships, a composite identity wherein the treasure within, the full development of the individual personality, is actualised in ways that enable the young to participate effectively in a rapidly changing and uncertain world. The concept of 'multiple citizenship' begins with an acceptance of the oneness of the human family and the interconnectedness of all nations, cultures and religions as we address global and regional problems. It implies, for example, that we should systematically seek to develop, through national education programmes, a passionate respect for the 'inherent dignity and equal and inalienable rights of all members of the human family' as the 'foundation of freedom, justice and peace in the world' (preamble to the Universal Declaration).

World citizenship does not imply an abandonment of legitimate national and cultural loyalties, nor the abolition of national autonomy, nor the imposition of uniformity. It does imply unity in diversity, internationally as well as nationally. As Gandhi stressed, understanding and respecting the culture and religion of others is possible only if one respects one's own cultural identity. While it is only to be expected that much of a country's education will focus on national languages, literature, history, rights and responsibilities, it must be conceded that current education systems tend to be too ethnocentric and nationalistic. In the twenty-first century, we will need to give much greater attention to developing an understanding of, and respect for, the richness and diversity of the world's cultures and ecosystems, to global issues, to universally accepted values, and to our rights and responsibilities as citizens of the world.

One of the important recent UNESCO reports, *Learning: The Treasure Within* (UNESCO 1996a), commonly referred to as the Delors Report, arose out of the International Commission on Education for the 21st Century, which included representatives from all regions, cultures and religions, and which received submissions and held hearings in all regions of the world. The Commission's recommendations present a refreshing reminder that education is about human values and cultures, about knowledge and commitments, about teachers and students – not just about markets, money and machines.

The Delors Report begins with an analysis of current tensions: between the global and local, the universal and the individual, tradition and modernity, long-term and short-term considerations, competition and equality of opportunity, the spiritual and the material. For the Commission members, designing and building our common future means 'a renewed emphasis on the moral and cultural dimensions of education, enabling each person to grasp the individuality of other people and to understand the world's erratic progression towards a certain unity: but this process must begin with self-understanding through an inner voyage whose milestones are knowledge, meditation and practice of self-criticism'. The report goes on to emphasise the need to adopt a long-term and participatory approach to education options, and to choose policies that establish the system's foundations based on common values and common goals (cf. Universal Declaration). The title conveys its central message: learning, that is, everything that humanity has learned about itself, is the treasure within the rich diversity of cultures which make up our global village. To find the treasure within, we must explore the accumulated wisdom, literature, knowledge and values of our own and many other cultures. Such an education must be a lifelong process, and be based on four pillars: *learning to know, learning to do, learning to live together* and *learning to be*. Learning to know involves combining reasonably broad general knowledge with the opportunity to study a small number of topics in depth and to develop the skills and motivation for learning to learn. Learning to do involves not only occupational skills but also the competence to deal with many situations and to work in teams. Learning to live together involves understanding others and their cultures, appreciating our interdependence and managing conflicts in the spirit of pluralism, mutual understanding and peace. Learning to be involves the full development of one's personality and the ability to act with ever greater autonomy, judgment and personal responsibility.

The Commission is critical of some formal systems and their overemphasis on the acquisition of knowledge (and, implicitly, the ways in which new technologies might lead to an emphasis on surfing the information highways to the neglect of learning to do, to live together and to be). It is vital, in its view, that we conceive of education in a more encompassing fashion, and take more seriously the broader social, cultural and moral objectives of education on which our common future depends. Such a vision should inform and guide educational reforms and policy in relation to both content and methods. The Commission reminds us that there are difficult choices to be made, but that the choices we make regarding equity, quality, curriculum, pedagogy and assessment define the type of global society we choose to become.

Whereas the Delors Report provides a broad framework for reflection and debate on the types of educational reforms needed to build a peaceful, pluralistic and democratic world society, UNESCO at a more practical level is seeking to articulate what this means in terms of educational policy, curriculum and teacher education programmes. In the course of doing so, it is publishing and disseminating reference materials in many languages to promote 'a culture of peace' and human rights. These materials were summarised in a recent report (UNESCO 1997) presented by the Secretary-General to the 1997 General Assembly.

At the 1994 International Conference on Education, Ministers of Education of the Member States of UNESCO approved a Declaration and Integrated Framework of Action on Education for Peace, Human Rights and Democracy which was formally adopted one year later (UNESCO 1995a). The Integrated Framework is concerned with: aims of education based on internationally agreed values; strategies, policies and lines of action; teaching materials and resources; programmes of teacher education; action on behalf of vulnerable groups; non-formal education; higher education; co-ordination of effort with family, media and other agents of socialisation, etc. The signatories promised: (1) to base their education systems on principles and methods that contribute to the building of respect for the human rights of others; (2) to strengthen the formation of values and abilities such as solidarity, creativity, civic responsibility and the ability to resolve conflicts by non-violent means; (3) to introduce into curricula education for citizenship which includes an international dimension; the ethical, religious and philosophical bases of human rights; their historical sources; national and international standards, such as the Universal Declaration of Human Rights; the basis of democracy and its various institutional models; the problem of racism and the history of the fight against sexism and all other forms of discrimination and exclusion; (4) to introduce curriculum reforms which emphasise knowledge, understanding and respect for the cultures of others; and (5) to link global problems to local action. If governments and their ministries meet their commitments and follow the guidelines which they approved, considerable progress can be made.

To help Member States meet their commitments, UNESCO has studied their policies and programmes, e.g. Teacher Training and Multiculturalism (UNESCO 1995b), monitored the extent to which they meet their legal obligations with respect to conventions like that on Discrimination in Education and, where necessary, drawn their attention to allegations of violations. It has also developed manuals to illustrate exemplary practice (e.g. UNESCO Kit on the Practice of Citizenship, Manual for Human Rights Education, Education for Tolerance, Language Education in Multi-cultural Societies); supported bilateral co-operation, NGOs and networks to promote the revision of school history and geography text-books, values education and civics education; promoted education for religious, cultural and linguistic pluralism; and linked schools serving violent communities. In addition, for more than 40 years, the Associated Schools Network has linked schools (currently about 5,000) from all regions (over 140 countries), and has serviced a grass-roots movement of teachers and students aimed at promoting international understanding and intercultural dialogue. It has also co-operated in the production of practical and innovative approaches to education. For example, the ASP 'Peace Pack' is presently being trialled in over 80 countries, and the World Heritage Educational Resource Kit for Teachers ('World Heritage in Young Hands'), which contains videos, CD-ROMs and materials developed by the schools on their heritage sites, will soon provide an attractive resource to promote appreciation of the richness and diversity of the world's cultures.

Promoting a culture of peace, based on mutual respect for the dignity of the individual and his or her culture, is most difficult in conflict situations. Under the Culture of Peace programme, UNESCO is trying to build peace in situations where there is a serious risk of conflict, or where there is, or has been, conflict.

Thus there is support for educational reconstruction, refugee education and education for conflict resolution in many places – Angola, Burundi, El Salvador, Guatemala, Kosovo, Mali, Mozambique, Rwanda and Somalia. In a small way, there is also support for activities that encourage integration and sharing between the young people from groups in conflict in Northern Ireland, Palestine and Israel, Turkey and Greece, and elsewhere.

A second source of reference stems from various international initiatives including the continuing emphasis on values, moral education and cultures in the Asia-Pacific region, and the creation of the APNIEVE network; the efforts made by the Council of Europe and the EU to build a European community and European citizens through education; the long-standing tradition in Scandinavian countries to stress respect for human rights and global, as well as national, citizenship; and the growing enthusiasm for national programmes as shown by the emergence of NGOs like CIVITAS, the establishment of the Academy for Democracy Education by Denmark, and various national projects now underway in Member States. With respect to the last, I will mention just two – the report of the Advisory Group on Citizenship from the United Kingdom (Crick 1998) and the Australian Discovering Democracy Schools Material Project (1997). The UK report declares that citizenship teaching should include 'the knowledge, skills and values relevant to the nature and practices of participative democracy; the duties, responsibilities, rights and development of pupils into citizens; and the value to individuals, schools and society of involvement in the local and wider community ... both national and local, and an awareness of world affairs and global issues, and of the economic realities of adult life'. The report identifies three strands which should, in its view, run through all education for citizenship: social and moral responsibility, community involvement and political literacy. It argues for producing active citizens equipped to have an influence in public life, and admits to a growing concern in many Western 'democracies' regarding the levels of 'apathy, ignorance and cynicism about political and public life and also involvement in neighbourhood and community affairs'.

As David Kemp stressed in 1997 in *Introducing the Discovering Democracy Schools Material Project*: 'Our education system is a vital means of maintaining the civil society and also in developing and enhancing our democratic system as we move to the next millennium. Effective democracy is not a static, inflexible concept, but a dynamic, active principle that needs to be continuously cultivated, adapted and revitalised.' By looking through the programmes and kits, I have learned a great deal about being an Australian, about the development of liberal and democratic ideas, institutions and legal frameworks in the US and the UK and their influence, as well as about the building of our own democratic institutions. As a scholar and teacher, I am pleased that support is being given to research, evaluation and professional development in designing the programme – far too often, such programmes are boring and off-putting to the young, and too rarely do they contribute to the development of values and patterns of behaviour which are their ultimate objective. As a world and Asia-Pacific citizen, however, I would like to see more emphasis being given to building democracy at the regional and global levels – to what I have called 'multiple citizenship'.

Conclusion

In all strategic actions, as the *World Education Report* (UNESCO 1998b) stresses, we need to take into account the critical role of the teacher in educating for a better future – remembering that what we do in our family, school and community life, what we watch on television, how we treat others and our attitudes towards other countries are far more powerful in shaping the values we pass on to our children than what we may choose to include in the curriculum.

We need to change our concepts and practices of power in schools, the workplace, and national and international politics from one based on force, self-interest and aggression to one based on respect for human rights and cultural differences, participation, consensus and non-violent social change. To do so will not be easy in a world accustomed to resolving conflicts by force – one in which national concerns and self-interest often triumph over the common good. If it has proved difficult for the Council of Europe to promote its programme for constructing European citizenship through education and training, we should not pretend that it will be easy to promote our international rights and responsibilities as 'world citizens'. Few curriculum guidelines have followed the example of Norway, which seeks to do so, and few school systems, other than the International Baccalaureat, will withhold their graduation certificates if community service requirements are not met.

Our common future will rest on whether we manage to educate ourselves throughout life for richness and diversity in a national and international context, in which the greatest threats to security, democracy and equity lie *within* societies. Together with partners like WEF, UNESCO is dedicated to helping our teachers and schools lay the foundations for peace, sustainable development and intercultural understanding. We have the vision and most of the tools needed to realise this goal: what is needed now is the political will.

References

Crick, B. 1998. *Education for Citizenship and the Teaching of Democracy in Schools*. Advisory Group on Citizenship from the United Kingdom, Final Report. Qualifications and Curriculum Authority: London.

Davis, W. 1999. The issue is whether ancient cultures will be free to change on their own terms. *National Geographic*, vol. 196, no. 2.

Fesl, E. 1987. Language death among Australian languages. *Australian Review of Applied Linguistics*, vol. 10, no. 2.

Introducing Discovering Democracy Schools Material Project. 1997. Curriculum Corporation: Carlton, Victoria.

UNICED. 1992. *Agenda 21*. United Nations Conference on Environment and Development. Conches.

UNESCO. 1948. *Universal Declaration of Human Rights*. UNESCO Publishing: Paris.

———. 1995a. *Declaration and Integrated Framework for Action on Education for Peace, Human Rights and Democracy*. UNESCO Publishing: Paris.

———. 1995b. *Our Creative Diversity*. Report of the World Commission on Culture and Development. UNESCO Publishing: Paris.

———. 1996a. *Learning: The Treasure Within* (Delors Report). Report of the International Commission on Education for the 21st Century. UNESCO Publishing: Paris.

———. 1996b. *Education for All Forum*. UNESCO Publishing: Paris.

———. 1997. *Towards a Culture of Peace*. UNESCO Publishing: Paris.

———. 1998a. *World Cultural Report*. UNESCO Publishing: Paris.

———. 1998b. *World Education Report: Teachers and Teaching in a Changing World*. UNESCO Publishing: Paris.

———. 1998c. *Universal Ethics Project*. UNESCO Publishing: Paris.

World Conference on Education for All. 1990. *World Declaration on Education for All*. Interagencies Commission: Jomtien, Thailand.

Three

A Working Consensus on a Desirable Future

An Australian Case-Study

℮⁓

Jack Campbell, Marilyn M. McMeniman,
and Nicholas Baikaloff

Nature of the Case-Study

The study reported here was undertaken as Stage I in a larger project aimed at devising educational curricula which would optimally serve the interests of both Australians and Australian society as we move into the twenty-first century. In addition to making a contribution at the national level, it was hoped that the mapping of concepts, clustering of goals and delineation of various goal-value systems would be useful to agencies such as UNESCO in their global discussions on 'our common future'.

Rather than tinker with existing curricula, it was decided to ask a select group of 250 community leaders to report on what kind of an Australian society they would like to see emerge in the foreseeable future. All of those approached occupied, or had recently occupied, State or national leadership positions in a variety of organisations, and a large percentage of them had been honoured for 'services to the community'. They included an ex-Governor General; leaders in such diverse fields as science, humanities, social sciences, agriculture, the creative arts, law, ethnic interests, urban design, business, union affairs, medicine, religion, community services, community development, trade, conservation, and education; as well as presidents of such community organisations as Rotary, Returned Services League, Gay/Lesbian Association and Country Women's Association. Almost all had been elected to their offices – the ex-Governor General is a notable exception, and he, before appointment, had held several very senior elected positions. Many of the 250 were household names throughout Australia, a few were known only to their own memberships; some were inspirational leaders who had initiated almost paradigmatic shifts in Australian thinking, others were low-key toilers furthering the causes of special interest groups. What they had in common was that they all spoke on behalf of some facet of Australian society and were involved in contributing to directions being taken by that society. Because of these two factors, their visions seemed to have special significance.

From the 250, a random sub-sample of 170 were approached and invited to participate in a four-phase study. On the completion of Phase 1 (an open-ended 'vision' statement), the other 80 were approached to join the initial sub-sample in Phases 2, 3 and 4. The aim of this design was to bring in a new group which would reflect upon, add to, delete from or otherwise amend the findings that were beginning to emerge, but were not yet set in concrete. Of the initial sub-sample, 81 responded with submissions, and, from the second sub-sample, 51 entered the study. Thus, the total response sample numbered 132 – 53 per cent of those who were approached. Given the nature of the research population (all of whom had extremely heavy commitments, often overseas), the burden of the tasks set and the need to maintain involvement over a six-month period, the response rate was considered very satisfactory. We appreciated this generous co-operation.

Most of the vision statements submitted were in conventional form, but a few were paintings, sketches or poems; some were brief and focused on a single theme, but others extended to 20 or more pages and provided a rich tapestry of thinking; some were in simple tabulated form, but others were highly polished submissions which showed evidence of several revisions. About one in five of the participants submitted, along with their response, copies of relevant articles which they had written and published earlier, and these were accepted as supporting submissions. All were serious attempts to address the issue of a desirable future for Australia.

On receipt of the 81 vision statements, an analysis was undertaken to identify major themes or 'goal-sets'. These were forwarded (Phase 2) to the 81 initial respondents and the 51 new entrants for comments and *ratings* of importance from 1 (low) to 10 (high). The annotations at this stage were almost as rich as the vision statements, and these were taken on board in Phase 3, when the 132 participants were asked to (a) reconsider their initial ratings in the light of (i) changes of wording in the goal-sets and (ii) ratings assigned by other participants, and (b) allocate *weightings* of importance to the revised goal-sets. At Phase 4, participants were presented with the final versions of the goal-sets, as well as the ratings and weightings, and were asked to structure the free-standing goal-sets into a system according to personal judgements concerning degree of permeation, overarching importance and the like (more details are available in Campbell, McMeniman and Baikaloff 1992).

Free-Standing Goal-Sets Extracted from the Vision Statements, Annotations, and Supporting Documents

An initial analysis of the 81 vision statements and supporting documents submitted by the first sub-sample led to the identification of 21 goal-sets. As a result of annotations at Phase 2, two of these were merged, and two more were added, giving a total of 22 which were retained in later stages of the Dephi exercise. The final ratings and weightings of importance ascribed to these 22 revealed a high measure of consensus with respect to 12 of them, and considerably less agreement on the importance of the remaining 10. Consequently, the intention here is to discuss only 13 – the distinct cluster of the top 12, plus one other (whose inclusion will be justified later). These are presented in the order of consensual strength (percentage of top ratings of 8s, 9s and 10s), and are followed by the explanations given by those who persisted in ascribing ratings which they knew were markedly lower than those allotted by the bulk of their fellow participants.

Just: *Australia should be a society which provides equal access to opportunities for all. It should be a place where all who wish can participate equitably in the social, cultural, recreational, economic and political life of the nation. Justice for all is paramount if we are to establish ourselves as a mature society.* (98 per cent)

As the percentage figure suggests, only a small number (three) of the participants declined to endorse this value strongly. These non-conformists claimed that the wording of the item did not do justice to the principles that (a) not all individuals have a right of access to everything (there may, for example, be limited opportunities, or prior conditions to be met) and (b) there need not be equal proportions of all groups enjoying the opportunities (different groups may have different preferences, if not abilities – witness, women in front-line battle units).

They were, however, prepared to accept that there should be no selection on *irrelevant* criteria, and that, when preconditions feature, 'affirmative' programs should be available to ensure that 'disadvantaged' groups experience genuine equality of access. Modification of the item to include these elements might well have resulted in 100 per cent endorsement at a high level – but we ran out of phases!

Sustainable Development: *The Australian society of the future should function within a policy of sustainable development – development which meets the needs of present generations without diminishing the resources of the world on land and in the air and sea. Such a policy has important implications for population rates, economic activities and the like. Australians of the future should be prepared to act appropriately on the basis of this knowledge.* (91 per cent)

The non-conformists had no great quarrel with the wording of the item – they were prepared to accept the notion of 'care and protection' of resources in the 'common sense' interests of this and subsequent human generations, but they suspected a 'hidden agenda' of a 'global community' which embraced all species, and they were not prepared to storm the barricades on behalf of poisonous red-back spiders, stone fish and the like! (This suspicion was unwarranted as there was another item – not so strongly supported – which addressed the issue of other species.)

Caring: *Australia should be a caring society in which all members are valued and respected irrespective of gender, race, colour or creed. It should be a compassionate one with special concern for the vulnerable and disadvantaged. Individuals should have a guaranteed sense of place in society.* (91 per cent)

Although ratings of this item ranged from 4 to 10, those participants (12) who used the band of 4 to 7, with a knowledge that the great majority of other participants were ascribing 8s, 9s and 10s, gave no explanation for their divergence.

Higher-Order Thinking and Knowing: *Individuals should be competent in analysing and asking the right questions, choosing, judging, discriminating, considering the human factors, ordering chaotic situations and dealing with ambiguity. They should be able to dispute, discuss, etc. in a rational way by weighing the arguments and arriving at conclusions in a disciplined, imaginative manner. They should be able to question, criticise and innovate, not from a position of ignorance or pure fancy but from one of well-based understanding.* (91 per cent)

As the percentage figure shows, this item was well supported by the great majority of participants. Among those who were less enthusiastic, a small number argued that: (a) it was unrealistic to expect *all* Australians to achieve competence in intellectual tasks such as these, (b) the item presented a typical Western view of 'scientific' thinking and (c) the item did not do justice to the element of 'inspired guesswork' which characterises good thinking, even in the sciences. There was a need for non-Western 'intuitive' approaches, as well as others that feature in such fields as the humanities, art and religion.

Empathic: *Australia should be a society in which individuals have developed capability in sympathetic imagination – understanding how other people are feeling, what they are thinking, why they act as they do and how they are conceptualising the world.* (89 per cent)

The non-conformists here argued that the mere development of empathy was insufficient – individuals must be prepared to proceed to more enlightened, caring, compassionate *actions* suggested by the heightened understanding. Empathy should not degenerate into consolation unaccompanied by action – in terms of Buddhist philosophy, *doku* (feeling the suffering of another) should develop into *bakku* (removal of the cause of suffering).

Open Global Relationships: *Australia should see itself as one nation among many and, through association with much broader and more general human contact, become intellectually enriched. The arid nationalism and parochial chauvinism of 'Australia-first-and-best' should give way to a more mature concept of international membership.* (89 per cent)

Once again, no comments were forthcoming from the non-conformists.

Regional Alignment: *Australians should learn to accept their geographic position as part of the Asia-Pacific region, and to relate to their neighbours without feeling either superior or inferior. There should be active involvement with the people of the region as one of them, though with a distinctive cultural background. Closer integration (psychological, cultural, social and economic) should develop without harm to traditional ties throughout the globe.* (88 per cent)

The alternative proposition advanced by those who assigned lower ratings was that Australia should be confident enough to aim simply at good relations with all regions of the world, that it should take an independent stand on international issues and achieve security through a commitment to promoting a 'world community' in a sensitively helpful manner, rather than through agreements with powerful friends. According to this view, a regional affiliation, if one exists at all, should be seen merely as a stepping-stone to a global affiliation and should not become a permanent arrangement: 'It is crucial to see any stage (for example, regionalisation) towards global relationships as a division which could produce antagonisms on a greater scale.'

Cultivation of Knowledge: *In addition to specialist knowledge, individuals should have a broad conceptual grasp of human and natural phenomena including science, technology, humanities, creative arts and other forms of knowledge. Knowledge should be seen in the context of the historical evolution of society, its present institutions and structures, and in relation to what goes on in other parts of the world. Knowledge specialists should understand the place of values and ethical issues in social and economic policy and in business and personal behaviour. In addition to knowing that and knowing how, individuals should be capable of integrating these in intelligent and competent performance.* (86 per cent)

Those who assigned low ratings of importance to this item objected to the perceived assumptions that: knowledge is good, and more knowledge is better; it is good for the sum total of knowledge to grow; the pursuit and attainment of knowledge are good; the simple fact of knowing is good. In their view, some knowledge is trivial and some is bad. Some respondents were unconvinced by appeals to a post-industrial and technocratic society, expressing concern that advances in scientific and technological knowledge were out of kilter with values and institutions. In their opinion, values have lost both their initiating and persistent power – they have become reactors to the more determinant technological developments, rather that proactors continually monitoring and influencing the growth and direction of these developments. Others were concerned that the view of knowledge being presented was a 'rationalist', Western kind, and did not do justice to indigenous and non-Western accumulations of wisdom. There was a need to take a much stronger multicultural view of knowledge.

Intellectually Driven Economy: *In contrast to past times, future wealth creation should flow more from invention and innovation. Future Australia should value and have greater recourse to the brains, creativity and inventiveness of both scientists and non-scientists. As a society, we should capitalise to a greater extent than currently on the rich linguistic and cultural resources of our multi-ethnic population.* (86 per cent)

As the percentage figure suggests, there was considerable support for the (then) Prime Minister's call for Australia to become 'the clever country', but among those who rejected this call were several who argued that Australian society was in danger of becoming 'trapped' by old concepts of work that were once appropriate but which were becoming increasingly inappropriate. There was a need for the development of a new, more humane concept of employment which would embrace home care and community services, giving status and dignity to those who, in a fiercely competitive market, might spend a lifetime on the dole. This new concept would encompass all activities associated with participation as a productive society member: 'The concept of success should change away from the individualistic notion of competing with fellow society members, winning and receiving a greater access to resources as a result. Success must come to mean that an individual contributes in an optimal way to the building of a strong community....'

Moral Responsibility: *Australians should progress to a higher level of moral responsibility as shown in higher standards of ethics within the business and wider community. The values of the 'me generation' and the 'decade of greed' should give way to those reflecting a higher sense of communal responsibility. Individual goals and aspirations should have regard to the needs and aspirations of others. The worship of materialism should decline.* (85 per cent)

At first glance, this item, like many others, must seem to be a 'motherhood' one, so it is salutary to note that, although consensus was high, there were ratings as low as 1! One of the participants who ascribed this low rating wrote as an annotation: 'In world-wide terms, one lesson of the collapse of the socialist regimes in Eastern Europe, of the crisis in China, and even of the re-establishment of Western supremacy following the decline of the Soviet Union and the Gulf War is that most people do not want to be equal. They want to get ahead of others. Although I used to doubt it, I now suspect strongly that this is so because of human nature and that it is both undesirable and futile to counter it beyond a certain point.'

Internationally Responsible: *A concept of global co-operation and involvement should emerge in a stronger form, and Australians should see themselves as world citizens. Australia should develop into an internationally responsible society which makes its own considered, independent and sensitive contribution to the building of a world community in which all people are free from threats of war, want and ecological disaster. It should contribute to overcoming poverty and oppression and should sensitively help 'developing' countries by providing aid, training and trade.* (85 per cent)

There were few objections to this value, although a small number of participants commented that Australia should address problems in its own patch (such as poverty and recriminations among indigenes) before distributing largesse overseas.

Co-operation: *Australia should be a co-operative society which harnesses the richness of individual and cultural diversity for the welfare of individuals and the community. We should learn a sense of community, of working together and of interdependence.* (84 per cent)

While giving some endorsement to this value, a number of respondents went on to add that there was a place for a measure of competition, that some degree of tension can be growth-promoting and valuable: 'While milk comes from contented cows, it is aggravated oysters that produce pearls!' 'To be totally co-operative implies the organisation of an ant colony. We need to accommodate the cranky, unco-operative innovators.' 'A healthy level of dispute and contestation of ideas and interests can prevent a society from stagnating intellectually and morally.'

The mean consensual percentage (88.6) of these 12 items is impressively high, although it would be naive to assume that everyone was interpreting them in precisely the same way.

Of the 10 items that had significantly lower consensual ratings, three related to Australia as a socially and culturally cohesive society; two sought a 'no-nonsense', 'hard-nosed', economically competitive society; two suggested a recycling of the 'familist' movement (strong primary groups of families and neighbourhoods) which was prominent in the period of post–Second World War reconstruction in Australia; one envisioned individuals with a stronger sense of personal control; one was concerned with developing a 'world community', embracing all species; and one focused on cultivation of the 'human spirit'. The mean consensual percentage of these 10 items was 70.3.

Reference was made earlier to the retention for future consideration of one of the lower-ranking items. This was *nurturance of the human spirit,* whose consensual percentage (57) was the lowest of all 22 goals:

Human Spirit: *The human spirit is the element in our search for meaning, our explorations of the unknown and our glimpse of the unity and interrelatedness of all components of what we know as the universe. It is the source of our universal values which go beyond the materialistic and the immediate and provide us with an inner reality, a flame, a mode of consciousness, a feeling of connectedness with the universe and, to some, a spark of divinity.*

The reason for retention of this 'spiritual' item, despite the low consensus associated with it, is threefold: first, whereas the other nine items in the 'low' cluster revealed a somewhat normal curve distribution of ratings, peaking around 5, 6 and 7, the *human spirit* attracted a bimodal distribution – many very low ratings and many very high ones, with few in between; second, those who assigned very low ratings were, nevertheless, highly supportive of a form of 'spirituality'; third, at the fourth and final phase, when participants were asked to structure their goal-sets into a values *system*, the human spirit featured in an overarching capacity to a greater extent than any single other.

Initially (Phase 2), the 'spirituality' item contained what was seen by some to be a strong religious element, with a reference to 'belief and faith', which appealed to church leaders and other committed Christians, in particular. As a result of the strong rejection of this element by a considerable number of participants, however, it was omitted at Phase 3, and the item was changed to 'human spirit'. The result was a similar distribution, but with high raters of spirituality tending to become low raters of human spirit, and low raters of spirituality becoming high raters of human spirit. The former of these shifts is evident in the following two extracts from annotations at Phase 3 (the first from a very senior Catholic Church leader, and the second from a Protestant social scientist):

> I am not sure what an item concerned with human spirit means. It can be interpreted as self-centredness and arrogant self-sufficiency that promotes greed and runs counter to almost all of the other goals that have emerged in the study. Man is totally dependent on, and subordinate to, God. It is in this relationship that he finds his own worth and identity.

> As a committed Christian, I cannot help but regret the lack of reference in Phase 3 to the powers which I believe create, maintain and support the human race – and all else. I feel that without some awareness and understanding of these powers – and attempts to align our society with them – our best endeavours will never reach the real heights, because they will be thwarted by human self-centredness and greed.

Clearly, although we had not succeeded in presenting a satisfactory item (again, we ran out of phases), an overwhelming number of participants wanted to retain *some* element of spirituality within the study. In the circumstances, we decided to retain *human spirit*, but to acknowledge a stronger religious component in subsequent explorations. This is demonstrated in Chapter 4, in which Oats presents an exemplar with a religious perspective, alongside one that lacks this characteristic.

Clustering and Structuring of the Goal-Sets

A statistical analysis (multidimensional scaling) of the 13 goal-sets that were retained in this study confirmed that five 'clusters' were identifiable:

1. A society that is committed to cultivating the essential nature of what it is to be human – item: *human spirit*.
2. A society that is committed to cultivating thinking and knowing in its individuals – items: *knowledge, higher-order thinking and knowing,* and *intellectually driven workforce skills.*

3. A society that espouses humane interpersonal relationships – items: *equitable treatment of all, care and compassion, empathy* and *co-operation*.
4. A society that is imbued with a strong sense of moral responsibility and concern for the common good – item: *moral responsibility*.
5. A society that is conscious of its global responsibilities – items: *sustainable development, open global relationships, regional alignments* and *international responsibilities*.

The final task set for the participants in the study (Phase 4) was to organise the clusters into a *system* which showed interrelationships, overarching importance and the like. As one would expect, many of the value systems that were submitted were highly idiosyncratic. Nevertheless, if only the five clusters mentioned above are considered, there was a large measure of support for a representation made up of four concentric circles: *human spirit* being the outmost, followed by *moral responsibility*, followed by *higher-order thinking and knowing*, and, then, at the core, *humane interpersonal relationships* and *global responsibilities*. We have called this the 'preferred' conceptualisation, simply because it surfaced most frequently. Clearly, it would have been better to have returned it to participants for endorsement, but this would have involved adding an unexpected phase at the end, and we thought it unwise to do that.

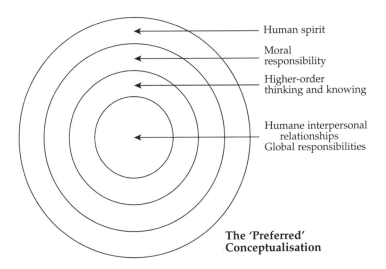

- Human spirit
- Moral responsibility
- Higher-order thinking and knowing
- Humane interpersonal relationships
- Global responsibilities

The 'Preferred' Conceptualisation

The 'preferred' conceptualisation shows the five clusters organised into a single system from regions of greater to lesser inclusiveness, and this is supported by accompanying statements such as these:

> The organisation of my goals is in clusters within one central goal which I would call 'cultivation of the human spirit'. I see this goal of paramount importance – so much so that I would rather not have it as a separate category. Rather, it is something which permeates all other goals. It is a life orientation, an undergirding characteristic, a master sentiment.

> The human spirit – the existential reality of what it means to be human, the sense of 'one-ness' of humans with this planet and the Universe – is, for me, ultimate.

> My inclination is to rank the goals according to the degree to which they enhance the distinctively human capacities of the individual, especially the capacity for 'transcendence', i.e. ability to distinguish oneself from the world, and encourage commitment to moral and interpersonal goods.

From a consideration of the diagram and the supporting statements, it could be concluded that the human spirit is understood by many to be the embodiment of distinctively human attributes – having a sense of moral responsibility, possessing and using capacities of higher-order thinking and knowing, being committed to humane interpersonal relationships and having a sense of global responsibility. The overall structural principle of the 'preferred' system, then, is what David Ausubel (1963: 53) called *derivative subsumption* – a person who understood this concept of human spirit would see the other clusters as implicit in, and representative of, it; they are self-evidently derivable. The relationships among all but the two most inclusive subsumers (human spirit and moral responsibility), however, appear to be more complicated. While moral responsibility can be regarded as being implicit within the human spirit, higher-order thinking and knowing is not self-evidently derivable from moral responsibility, and neither are humane interpersonal relationships and global responsibility self-evidently derivable from higher-order thinking and knowing, alone. Rather, within an overarching human spirit, higher-order thinking and knowing is an addition to moral responsibility, and the relationship between the two, then, is one of *correlative subsumption*. Similarly, humane interpersonal relationships and global responsibility are *correlatively* subsumed within higher-order thinking and knowing because they are not directly derivable from the latter, but are selective objects of it. Australians are being asked to nurture higher orders of thinking and knowing, not as ends in themselves, but, when combined with the correlative sense of moral responsibility, as *means to* more humane interpersonal relationships and stronger global responsibilities. It is this somewhat complex mixture of derivative and correlative subsumptions which, in this case, converts a mere 'shopping list' into a system.

As shown earlier, the interpretation of the 'preferred' ordering of the goals, which is presented in the paragraph above, can be supported by extracts from several of the vision statements and annotations. One vision statement, in particular, appears to represent the total very well, and we reproduce it, in its entirety, below. (It also gives readers a good example of the 'raw' data available to us.)

Personal Vision Statement: Richard Bawden

'The thinking that has brought us to this stage cannot carry us beyond it.'
Albert Einstein

I dream of an Australia where individuals, families, schools, professional groups, business organisations, bureaucracies and universities, etc. are committed to the inexorable process of self-renewal – of creative learning for transforming relationships. I dream of an Australia which is known and respected throughout the world for the quality of the ways by which its people treat each other and their visitors, and deal with their own environments. In such a vision, I see new ways of thinking and envisioning, encouraging new ways of being: being productive, being appreciative, indeed, being, in the greatest sense of that word.

We are all aware of the need for a re-conceptualisation of our geopolitical alliances as well as our own regional identity. The need for a more proactive and collaborative self-reflexive exploration of ourselves as a unique civilisation is perhaps less well accepted. Yet this, I believe, should be our national focus.

My future Australia deals with its internal and external challenges in a far more creative, collaborative, holistic and responsible manner than is currently obvious: where progress is assessed for its dimensions of social aesthetics, cultural feasibility, social justice and ethical responsibility, as well as its individuality, utility and economic productivity. My future Australia will have a tolerant, appreciative, enviable commitment to the pursuit of quality in everything that it does. It will be an enterprising culture with a population keen to contribute to better ways.

We will be rethinking our business strategies and corporate structures, and our constitution and government practices; we will be exploring the effective management of our wastes as well as responsible land use practices; we will be rethinking urban and rural planning processes, collaborative work practices and trading relationships; above all else, we will be committed to forms of human rights and social justice we have yet to imagine.

Like all visions, mine are as grand as they appear idealistic; yet they are possible. Over the last decade or so, my colleagues and I have been participating with others in a remarkable process of rethinking of life and work in rural Australia. With movements like Landcare and Total Catchment Management, we are seeing systemic thinking and practices helping rural people come to terms with ethical development. We are seeing how innovative curricula, embracing 'methodological pluralism' and 'epistemological heterogeneity', can play a fundamental role in this context. My 'grand strategic plan' for educational systems in this regard will see major sponsorships provided for action research into innovative curricula: curricula which will release creativity and enterprise, and encourage its application to both personal praxis and a civilisation as we want it. It will see a focus on the learner and will display a total commitment to the equality of access, by all, to lifelong learning resources. It will see science, the fine arts and the humanities in a glorious synergy; the secular united with the spiritual; reflection with action; holism with reductionism.

... It is the world and me both that I want to improve, to change what was and what is to what could be and should be from the perspective of that which is in the common good and is ultimately ethically defensible.

In the conceptualisation above, *higher-order thinking and knowing* occupies a pivotal position. More than a quarter of a century ago, John Bremer (1973: 30) commented: 'In the past, knowledge has been treated as if it were a private possession ... more and more, [it] is seen as a mode of service to the public, to the community.' Bremer's statement might well have been one of hope more than of fact, for the 1989 UNESCO Report felt it still necessary to make a strong plea for this shift in role to occur: 'The new epistemology of knowledge and learning needs to include a change from emphasizing the private benefits of learning, to emphasizing the public benefits of learning. We need to develop a sense of service and to stress community benefit and the advancement of public good' (UNESCO 1989: 5). Much the same plea was made by participants in this study.

Conclusion

Although the participants in this study were asked to identify the *societal* characteristics which they would like to see in Australia, most quickly moved to a consideration of the characteristics that they would like to see in *individuals*. In support of this shift, two wrote:

> Reference is made to the kind of Australian society we should be developing. I would want a more fundamental approach, viz. what kind of Australian should we be developing, for the quality and nature of Australian society will be determined by the quality and character of the individuals who will shape that society.

> It has been necessary to establish that the development of the human individual is the hub of the enterprise. A warped self will warp all other levels of interaction and subvert the goals of social reformers.

By arguing in this manner, participants showed affinity with Rousseau, rather than Plato, but they were not advocating *blatant* individualism; rather, individual excellence was seen as a continuum which culminated in a commitment to fostering the 'common good'. The truly autonomous individual was to be an integral element within the social fabric, holding it together by the threads of personal morality. Self-eclipse, in this sense, does not entail self-elimination. As Garrison (1997: 66) has said: 'Self-eclipse … means that the present, relatively stable self is open to new possibilities for growth. Self-eclipse is not a passive activity; it creates its own expansive experience in conjunction with others.'

The goals which have emerged in this study may be regarded as 'transcendent' ones, with the Australian society being urged to create a world worthy of humans. Herein lies the opportunity for, and challenge to, education because, as Huebner stated (1985: 65), 'Everyone experiences, and continues to have the possibility of experiencing, the transcending of present forms of life, of finding that life is more than is presently known or lived. This is what education is about. Education is only possible because the human being is a being that can transcend itself.'

References

Ausubel, D.P. 1963. *The Psychology of Meaningful Verbal Learning.* Grune and Stratton: New York.

Bremer, J. 1973. *On Educational Change.* National Association of Elementary School Principals: Arlington, Virginia.

Campbell, J., McMeniman, M.M. and Baikaloff, N. 1992. *Visions of a Future Australian Society: Towards an Educational Curriculum for 2000 AD and Beyond.* Ministerial Consultative Council on Curriculum: Brisbane.

Garrison, J. 1997. *Dewey and Eros: Wisdom and Desire in the Art of Teaching.* Teachers College, Columbia University: New York.

Huebner, N.E. 1985. Spirituality and knowing. In E. Eisner (ed.). *Learning and Teaching: The Ways of Knowing.* University of Chicago Press: Chicago.

UNESCO. 1989. *International Symposium and Round Table.* Final Report. UNESCO Publishing: Paris.

— Four —

Nurturing the Human Spirit

William N. Oats

Introduction

The previous chapter reports that in the 1992 Campbell, McMeniman and Baikaloff study, many participants ascribed overarching value status to the *human spirit*. But what, precisely, is the *human spirit*? In a famous passage in Book II of his *Confessions*, St Augustine comments on the difficulty that one has in defining the widely used concept of *time*: 'What then is time?… If no one asks me, I know; but if I want to explain it to a questioner, I do not know.' Much the same is true for the human spirit. It might not be as commonplace as time, but I have been struck by the way it keeps appearing in the most unexpected places. A television advertisement hailed the award-winning film *An Angel at My Table* as 'an affirmation of the human spirit'; a New York paper reported Peter Garrett, of *Midnight Oil* fame, as saying that he saw his music as a means of expressing his faith in the spirit within; it is the thread running through Caroline Jones's ABC series *Search for Meaning*, and less explicitly in Manning Clark's *Quest for Grace*. This suggests that, though we cannot easily define it, the human spirit is the element of our inward search for meaning, even if that search is subconscious, as it was for Patrick White's protagonists – *Explorers of the Interior*. It features in Bryce Courtney's *The Power of One* (1989: 22): 'The beginning of the Power of One is where I would learn that in each of us there is a flame that must never be allowed to go out, that as long as it burns within us we can never be destroyed.' There is the testimony, too, of one who works on the frontiers of modern science, Fritjof Capra (1988: 113): 'Spirituality, or the human spirit, could be defined as a mode of consciousness in which we feel connected to the cosmos as a whole. Ecological awareness is spiritual in its deepest sense.'

Paul Davies (1990), another physicist, introduces an element of divine involvement, design and purpose when he carries this sense of awareness into the whole field of science and mathematics with such observations as 'There is some God-like force at work in Nature', and the feeling that 'the world seems amazingly ingenious, in some ways "contrived", and that humans have a part to play in that'. He is moved by a sense of wonder. This comes out very forcefully in Wayne Crawford's interview with him, as reported in the Hobart *Mercury* of 25 March 1995:

> What I'm talking about is whether there is an underlying meaning or purpose in the universe. The weight of evidence from science points to a design. If we look at the underlying laws of physics, the ingenuity, the harmony, when they are put together is suggestive of some deeper meaning – something that involves us in some way.... The universe is not only ordered, it is intelligibly ordered.... We live in a wonderful universe, rich and interesting. We are part of that miracle. Has the universe conspired to have us in it?... The miracle is nature itself, that it can give rise to the complexity and the life and the consciousness – and then consciousness develops to the point where we can actually uncover these laws. It is an incredible story.

The human spirit is not identical with religious spirituality but, by the same token, it does not exclude this perspective. Many will agree with Brian V. Hill when he states (1992: 46):

> ... the question of the source and animation of these [distinctively human] capacities is left open, though if students are to have an adequate understanding of human behaviour we also owe it to them to provide opportunities at some point in the curriculum to study the reflective traditions, especially religious, which have sought to answer such questions.

Again like time, the human spirit finds its witness in metaphor rather than in definition, in poetry rather than in dissertation. But the clearest evidence for the reality of the human spirit is to be found in the lives of those human beings in whom this spirit has struggled for expression and recognition. Surely this was the source of Socrates' willingness to drink the cup of hemlock rather than betray what he called his 'inner god', and, also, the 'inner voice' which Gandhi said had urged him to lead his people to freedom without recourse to violence. This, too, was the source of the dream of Martin Luther King Jr which called him to walk up the mountain of his vision even though this meant the assassin's bullet, and of Nelson Mandela's long and tortuous 'march to freedom'. But the richest evidence of all, I find, is in the person of that intriguing, elusive, yet compelling figure of Jesus of Nazareth. He, like so many other explorers of the potential of the human spirit, has suffered at the hands of those who would exalt him by enshrining him in an institution and encasing his inspiring life and teachings in a mesh of dogma and ritual. Jesus of Nazareth, the human being, not Jesus the Christian enthroned by the Church, represents one of those great leaps in the evolution of the human spirit, and deep within each one of us is this evolutionary potential. We may not share the fame of those mentioned above, but we, too, are of their kind and can share their immortality, cherishing the faith they strengthen within us that:

> Enough, if something from our hands have power
> To live, and act, and serve the future hour;
> And if, toward the silent tomb we go,
> Through love, through hope, and faith's transcendent dower,
> We feel that we are greater than we know.
>
> Wordsworth, 'After-Thought'

No distinctive culture, no self-appointed religious cult has proprietary claims of possession or exclusive rights of dispensation. The human spirit has outlasted all attempts by autocratic tyrants, political ideologists and arrogant materialists to deny or suppress it. It strives for expression, but rebels against dictation and dogma. It can stand the searching light of reason, but it relies upon its own intuitive powers of imagination to guide it through the surrounding darkness beyond the reach of reason's searchlight.

While we cannot assume that the human species is unique in the cosmic order of things, we can at least acknowledge that our humanity is a marvellous compound of distinctive attributes – reason, creativity, imagination, explorative curiosity, search for meanings, empathy, feelings of compassion, awareness of connectedness with the other components of the living planet, and god-like 'apprehension' – an innate awareness of that which is beyond the immediate and the observable. In creating our common future, nurturance of the human spirit should loom large among our priorities. As Palmer wrote very recently (1999: 6):

> I am passionate about not violating the deepest needs of the human soul, which education does with some regularity. As a teacher, I have seen the price we pay for a system of education so fearful of things spiritual that it fails to address the real issues of our lives – dispensing facts at the expense of meaning, information at the expense of wisdom. The price is a school system that alienates and dulls us, that graduates young people who have had no mentoring in the questions that both enliven and vex the human spirit.
>
> ... I advocate any way we can find to explore the spiritual dimension of teaching, learning and living. By 'spiritual' I do not mean the credal formulations of any faith tradition, as much as I respect those traditions and as helpful as their insights may be. I mean the ancient and abiding human quest for connectedness with something larger and more trustworthy than our egos – with our own souls, with one another, with the worlds of history and nature, with invisible winds of the spirit, with the mystery of being alive.

The intention in the next section is to show how two schools which have had a commitment to nurturing the human spirit have gone about their educational task. The first has had a non-religious orientation (at least in the traditional credal sense), while the second is steeped in Quaker principles. By presenting these two contrasting perspectives, it is hoped that justice will be done to the bimodal distribution of ratings which was referred to near the end of Chapter 3.

Two Exemplars

L'Ecole Internationale (Ecolint)

In September 1938, when Europe was on the brink of the Second World War, and again in August 1949, I was privileged to begin two-year periods of teaching at l'Ecole Internationale, Ecolint for short, in Geneva. This school has special significance in the history of the World Education Fellowship (Ligue Internationale pour l'Education Nouvelle), for it was established in 1923 by Adolphe Ferrière, one of the founders and central figures of the Fellowship, in part to demonstrate how the principles of the Fellowship might be implemented. It is also of special significance within the confines of this chapter, since among the seven principles which were adopted by the Ligue at Calais in 1921, two (Nos. 1 and 2) make direct reference to the nurturance of the human spirit, and a third (No. 7) makes implicit reference:

1. The essential goal of all education is to prepare the child to aim at, and to realise in his own life, the supremacy of the spirit; hence, whatever particular points of view may be involved, education must strive to preserve and to increase spiritual energy in the child.
2. It must respect the child's individuality, which can be developed only by a training that furthers the expression of the spiritual forces within him....
7. New education fits the child to become not only a citizen capable of fulfilling his obligations to his near ones, to his country, and to all mankind, but also a human being conscious of his worth as man.

Two further points of some relevance are that, between my two periods of teaching, Ecolint and its graduates had undergone a testing of the human spirit as the war in Europe raged around them, and, during my second term (1949), I conducted a study among the school's *anciens* in which I asked them what had been the chief influence of Ecolint on their outlook and development. These four factors—association with WEF, the deep concern of Ecolint with nurturing the human spirit, the school's actions during the war and the responses of former pupils relating to the influence of Ecolint—combine to make Ecolint a very appropriate exemplar for presentation here. The fact that the report relates to events of more than 50 years ago seems to be of little significance.

When I was first appointed to Ecolint, there were 187 students of 27 nationalities in attendance. The Americans and the Swiss led the field with 32 each, Great Britain contributed 26, Germany 19, China 17. The Chinese group was a fascinating one. Some years previously, a wealthy Chinese philosopher had come to Geneva and had been so impressed with the School and its philosophy that he decided he would educate the future leaders of his country at Ecolint. He returned to China, selected (by what methods I do not know) a group of ten 5- to 6-year-olds, shipped them off to Geneva, where they arrived knowing neither French nor English and doubtless unaware of the reason for their sudden transition to an entirely foreign culture. By 1938 they were in the senior part of the school, but, alas, the tides of war had swept over their homeland and they were now international refugees.

How successful was Ecolint in nurturing the human spirit? Perhaps one answer is contained in the editorial of the June 1940 edition of the school magazine, *Ecolint*, which reached me and 12 British and American charges at Hendaye, on the escape route from Bordeaux to England:

> In spite of the torment the International School will not betray its traditions. This is why this magazine, *Ecolint*, appears.... Life in Europe is difficult. One after the other our hopes have collapsed in ruins; our great ideal of international understanding and friendship seems to have disappeared. But this is only on the surface. This great net, which Ecolint has stretched around the world, can in no way be torn apart. Whatever happens we have friends under all flags and the fluctuations of politics cannot break such bonds. At this moment a world is dying. It has some good aspects and some bad. Let's not mourn its passing. We are young.... A new world is being born. The future is ours, the young. You, our friends in all countries around the globe, we, the students now at school, we must draw closer together, elbow to elbow. By our understanding, by our effort, we shall furnish the framework on which shall be woven the world of tomorrow.

The school kept that faith alive, 'in spite of the torment', in spite of the reign of violence and smoke of the gas ovens. Ecolint survived (itself a major achievement) and its doors were thrown open to refugees from that terror. One of them, Marianne Schwarz, later a professor of French at the University of Maryland, US, wrote: 'Thanks to my friends at Ecolint I was able to take the shock of the message that came to me, black on white, that my parents had perished at Auschwitz.'

Another answer is given in the responses to the 1949 survey of former students referred to earlier. Among the main contributions attributed to Ecolint was that of building and sustaining *foi en l'homme* – faith in humanity: 'If my despair is not total, it is thanks to the spark of faith which the School kept alive and which remains with me in spite of the torment.' The responses reminded me of an idea which is so beautifully expressed by Antoine de St Exupéry in his *La Terre des Hommes*: 'Etre homme, c'est précisément être responsable ... c'est sentir en posant sa pierre que l'on contribue à bâtir le monde' (To be a man is precisely to be responsible ... it is to feel that in placing one's stone, one is contributing to building the world).

A third measure of Ecolint's success is to be found in the fact that, following a UNESCO-sponsored meeting in Paris in 1949, this school was chosen as the venue for a three-week summer course for teachers interested in international education. Participants in the course represented a whole spectrum of experience, ranging from young teachers in training to the most renowned of European educationists. Eighteen nationalities were represented, Great Britain topping the list with nine participants, then Germany with seven, Italy and the US with five each, an interesting group from India, Pakistan and Ceylon, and also one from the Scandinavian countries. This conference was, I believe, the foundation for the development of the Association of International Schools. Ecolint throughout has played a key role in this Association, providing not only much of the inspiration, but also mentors with highly regarded practical experience.

How did Ecolint achieve its widely acknowledged success? The school had a formidable academic reputation in the French Baccalaureat, Swiss Maturite, Oxford and Cambridge, American College Board and Australian Matriculation examinations, but examinations did not tyrannise either the curriculum or the school timetable. In fact, there were exciting opportunities for participation in music, theatre, art and sport, as well as the most demanding academic disciplines. I would hazard a guess that few schools could boast such a rich fare of theatre as Ecolint. It was not just a case of one school play a year; in my first year, Maeterlinck's *L'Oiseau Bleu*, Obe's *Noe*, Bernard Shaw's *Saint Joan*, Euripides' *Electra*, and several one-act plays were staged.

A variety of school activities provided means of promoting an excellent rapport between staff and students. Senior and Middle School Councils controlled much of the school's extracurricular activities and gave students scope for developing a sense of responsibility. A school paper, *The Amoeba*, its name suggesting that the school was a microcosm of the international community of the future, gave opportunities for a range of good-natured comment on daily school life and for creative writing.

At Ecolint, morning assemblies were the focal point of each day's community life. There was no religious ritual, for the school had no religious affiliations and there were as many religions represented as there were nationalities – but the assemblies had what was for me a religious significance. They upheld what was felt to be of value, what was humane. The lapsed Quaker radical Tom Paine was close to the truth that was sounded in these assemblies: 'The world is my country, my religion to do good.' Each morning's assembly had a theme – a commentary by a competent analyst of world affairs, a music recital, a talk on some subject of scientific interest, a student council report, a class presentation such as a short play – and on Saturdays there was a long assembly, which allowed for a variety of programmes, often given by celebrities visiting Geneva.

As stated in Chapter 1, the central theme of this book is the urgent need for humans to establish 'unity in diversity'. This was the driving force of much of Ecolint's programme, and, at the end of the school year in July 1950, I was fortunate to be co-ordinator and conductor of a festival with that title: *Unity in Diversity*. The production was a joint effort of students and staff, the result of a pooling of ideas and constant readjustment as yet another bright idea surfaced. We opened with a song and a joining of hands. Then national songs and dances followed, beginning with the host nation, the Swiss, themselves a demonstration model of 'unity in diversity' with Italian, French, German and Romanche each contributing their own individual and diverse flavour to the Swiss *mélange* of nationalities. Negro spirituals, work songs, cowboy songs, square dancing and a Mexican hat dance illustrated diversity within the Americas. 'La Famille Britannique' was no less diverse with the Welsh 'David of the White Rock' sung to harp accompaniment, the Skye Boat Song, the Canadian 'Alouette', the English 'Flowers of the Valley' – and for Australia, what else but 'Waltzing Matilda', acted with much gusto and with the jumbuck sporting a real sheepskin coat! Scene after scene illustrated our theme, with French, German, Italian, Dutch, Scandinavian, Indian, Russian, Hungarian and Greek participants all contributing in singing and dancing. We concluded, as we began, with a rousing marching song, each verse gathering the strength of numbers, ten comrades, arm in arm, heart to heart, a hundred, a thousand, a hundred thousand, and why not all humanity marching with triumphant step in peace? Somehow the festival was just right, for it summed up the *Esprit Ecolint*. The setting itself was perfect – with the open-air theatre, the children gathered on the grass behind the open stage, the parents seated under the trees and joining in with the songs when they wanted to. Everything was beautifully informal. Families wore national costumes, with Indian saris, Scottish kilts, Chinese robes all adding to the colour of the occasion.

On first encounter, it might be thought that the festival was just another instance of highlighting national differences, and likely to be divisive rather than unifying. As some of the participants in the visions study (reported in Chapter 3) stated, it is important that strong national and regional affiliations should not impede movement towards international citizenship. In Ecolint's case, there was no impediment; on the contrary, events such as the festival appeared to enhance feelings of self-worth, and these feelings enabled the students to broaden their affiliations to encompass people of all nationalities. Certainly, the former students referred often to this broadening of affiliation.

> Yes, the School did change some of my prejudices, for it took from me the feeling of inferiority which I'd had from being regarded by other nationals as a 'sale Boche' at a time when I could not have a clear attitude to such things myself. (a German girl)

> I certainly appreciated these international friendships at a time when it was normal to hate such and such nations. (a French boy)

> Seeing others as human beings and not classifying them according to nation, colour, religion or class. The strongest influence of the School on me is that I cannot, as the people around me do, hate the Germans, and I haven't been able to rejoice when atomic bombs have fallen on Japan. For me Japan is not a far-distant country but the home of the most beautiful girl of my year at Ecolint. – Kasu Sagimura (a British boy)

It will be obvious from the above that Ecolint offered an extraordinarily rich curriculum for the times, but Ecolint was more than its rich curriculum. Indeed, it was more than the sum of all its parts. In the survey of two thousand former students, many expressed appreciation of the contribution of bilingualism, world history and world geography to their outlook and development, and, particularly, of the cultural enlightenment of the daily assemblies, but they came back to something more fundamental than any of these. One said, 'I became conscious of the world as a whole, and how interrelated it is, and how basically alike are people of all nations.' Another commented, 'This community of nations was created almost imperceptibly in spite of oneself, and one realised in a remarkably short time this interdependence without friction.' What was more important than particular aspects of the curriculum was the *Esprit Ecolint*. Teachers, no less than students, experienced the influence of this difficult-to-define phenomenon. For me, it was as if a window was opening on a whole new and exciting vista – something like the grand breathtaking view I had when I first climbed the Saleve, an

Acropolis-like mountain just over the border near Geneva, and lifted my eyes, first to the Jura mountains beyond the Lake of Geneva, and then, with a hundred and eighty degrees' sweep, to the grand massif of Mont Blanc.

The Friends' School, Hobart

The Friends' School is a co-educational school, with 1,180 students from kindergarten to Year 12, situated in Hobart, in the south of Tasmania. It was founded in 1887 by Quakers from England, and though it is run under the auspices of Quakers, fewer than 5 per cent of the students and teachers at the School are Quakers. Striking features of this school are the clear statement of goals (*Purpose and Concerns*), the focus on values and the commitment of the staff and students to ensuring that these values are reflected in everything associated with the school. I was Headmaster of this school from 1945 to 1973, but I have asked my daughter, Dr Stephanie Farrall, a past student and present Co-Principal, to write about The Friends' School as it is today. Her account follows.

A central concern of The Friends' School has been to define the values of the School and to put these beliefs into action in the daily life of the School. We have focussed especially on the kind of community we would like to be, and on the way students and staff respect and value each other and their work. In this we see a link with 'learning to live together' and 'learning to be', two of the four pillars of education identified in the Delors Report to UNESCO, and referred to by Colin N. Power in the second chapter of this book.

A significant step in identifying the School's values came as a result of strategic planning in 1989. After an intensive process of consultation with members of the school community about our goals, the Board drafted a statement, *Purpose and Concerns*, which was adopted as the equivalent of a 'mission' statement.

Purpose and Concerns: The Friends' School is a co-educational Quaker school based on fundamental values such as the intrinsic worth of each person, the recognition of 'that of God' in everyone, the desirability of simplicity and the need to establish peace and justice. As a learning community, we are concerned for the academic, cultural, physical, social and spiritual development of each person in our care. We seek to help our students develop into men and women who will think clearly, act with integrity, make decisions for themselves, be sensitive to the needs of others, be strong in service and hold a global perspective. We believe that these aims can best be achieved with the active support of all members of our school community.

The term 'concerns' was chosen very consciously in order to link with the Quaker usage, which denotes something of deep importance coming from a clear leading of the spirit. 'Concerns' are closely associated with values, with what we hold important enough to act upon.

The *Purpose and Concerns* statement draws attention to the spiritual basis of our values by placing at the head of the list 'the intrinsic worth of each person' and 'the recognition of "that of God" in everyone'. These are understood to be two ways of expressing the same concept. It's essentially about recognising a universally human quality – the spiritual dimension, the light, the guiding or motive force, integrity, deep awareness, the sense of rightness, the impulse to locate the centre. It can't be defined rationally or in terms of the physical senses, yet it is sensed in a deeper way. We are on a life journey searching for the meaning of God in our own lives and encouraging those around us in our journey. In every lesson there is some way we are reaching out to the worth in each child, the awakening of the [human] spirit.

The statement also identifies other values which Quakers have traditionally held to be central – simplicity and commitment to peace and justice.

The *Purpose and Concerns* statement is under continual review and is used widely by the Board, staff, students and parents in guiding policies and practice. It has been the basis, for example, of the drug policy, classroom management policy, the curriculum statement, community service, and statements such as those about expectations of teachers and students, bullying, and students' rights and responsibilities. The challenge of continuing to clarify the values has been taken up in four significant ways in recent years: the establishment of a strategic planning group on values, the formulation of a five-year plan with values explicitly listed among the goals, professional development seminars on values and a staff planning group on school culture.

One example of how we are working to put our beliefs into action is through holding weekly silent 'Gatherings' in each part of the School, during which students and staff come together for an extended period of stillness and quiet reflection. Gatherings are an attempt to put into action our belief in the importance of nurturing the caring, reflective part of each child, of tending and attending to the spirit within each person. Gatherings are modelled on the Quaker experience of silent worship, but are modified in ways that attempt to cater for the needs of children and young people, the great majority of whom, as mentioned above, do not come from Quaker families.

Gatherings may be structured around themes, with both students and teachers contributing. Junior School students, for example, have recently led Gatherings on the themes of friendship and of dealing with conflict and exclusion. Year 10 students have spoken of the impact of seeing the film about the Dalai Lama, *Kundun*, and Year 7 students have shared their prayers for the twenty-first century after reading John Marsden's *Prayer for the 21st Century*. Gatherings for the oldest children (Years 11 and 12) resemble more closely a traditional Quaker Meeting for Worship, with groups of 50 to 80 students and teachers gathering in silence for 30 minutes, with no planned structure. People may speak out of the silence if they feel led to do so.

We chose the term 'Gathering' very carefully, as a welcoming, including term. We wanted students to feel at home in the silence, to feel that they could enter in their own way, find comfort and inspiration when they needed it, as well as relief from the pressures of having to perform, articulate and produce something. We hoped that Gatherings might provide an opening for them to share, out of their silence, insights and experiences on a level that may not be possible elsewhere.

In introducing weekly Gatherings, we have built on the significant role that silence has traditionally played in the life of The Friends' School. Assemblies have always started and closed with a period of silence, which falls unannounced. Classes in the Junior School start each day with a period of silence. The High School introduced the term 'Reflective Silence', and encouraged students to reflect at the end of each Assembly about the theme or the words of a visiting speaker.

Other examples of ways in which values are expressed through the life of the School are: End-of-Year Gatherings, Friendly Conferences and school productions. End-of-Year Gatherings have replaced the traditional speech night, and themes have expressed concerns coming from students and staff. Thus, one End-of-Year Gathering was held in the spirit of the Year of Indigenous People, through poetry, movement and music inspired by the words of Tasmanian Aborigines. Another End-of-Year Gathering was a celebration of peace and reconciliation in South Africa. A special message was sent to the people of South Africa in the form of a Book of Greetings and goodwill from the 'gathered community of The Friends' School', created by students and staff, and signed by everyone present. In a similar spirit, a 'Sorry Book' was prepared and presented to Ida West, a Tasmanian Aboriginal elder, in a special Whole School Gathering of commitment to reconciliation.

Friendly Conferences have been held every two years to give older students (Years 10, 11 and 12) an opportunity to explore a theme together over a whole day by listening to keynote speakers and taking part in workshops. The conferences are organised by a committee of students and staff who have chosen themes which are strong statements about the values of the School: 'Living in the World Together', 'Beliefs and Thoughts into Action', 'Conflict – Causes, Consequences, Cures', 'Creating a Friendly Future' and 'Let Your Lives Speak'.

Community seminars on themes such as 'Contemporary Aboriginality', 'An Introduction to Quakerism' and 'An Evening with Caroline Jones: Finding Meaning in Everyday Life' have enabled parents, staff and friends to explore issues closely related to the values of the school. A seminar on 'Our Family Future', with Steve Biddulph as one of the speakers, focused on issues such as better family communication and the changing roles of men and women in today's society.

The school's last two musical productions provide good examples of activities which reinforce the values of the school. Music and lyrics were written by staff and students and were special Friends' creations. *Wapping*, set in the historic working class district of Hobart in the last century, explored themes of the gap between the 'haves' and the 'have-nots', courage in facing hardship, the generation gap, and the idealistic dreams of youth. For *Visions of Vietnam*, students helped to research, write and perform a dramatic presentation on the war in Vietnam, by interviewing Australians and Vietnamese involved in the fighting and the peace movement. It was profoundly moving to watch students bring to life experiences of the war, and to feel their compassion for Vietnamese and Australians caught up in the moral dilemmas created by those experiences.

The School seeks to nurture and develop the imagination and capacity of students for empathy in other ways, as well: by exposing them to different cultures and religious traditions in a way that expands their understanding and helps them to see through the eyes of people of other cultures and faiths; by providing opportunities for students to enter imaginatively into the experiences of other people so that they can develop a concern for others, and show compassion and respect; by, for example, studying literature, Aboriginal Studies, Asian Studies, and Languages Other Than English.

The Friends' School has been very conscious of the fact that although classrooms can be effective settings within which to *learn about* values, a commitment to these is dependent upon experience of them throughout the total learning environment. Everything that is done, written and said conveys the values of a school: the way members treat each other and speak to each other, the formal curriculum, the co-curriculum, the 'hidden' or 'implicit' curriculum, the pastoral care structure, the way the school is administered, the activities, and the teaching methods that are adopted.

The Friends' School, no less than others, is heavily reliant on the quality of its teachers. We believe that as part of their professional role, teachers exert a powerful influence simply by 'being'. As Sichel (1988: 25) states: 'Teachers are not just facilitators or leaders of moral discussions or Socratic midwives, but serve as models for students.... Teachers influence student morality by the persons they are, how they act, how they relate to a student, what they say, how and what they teach, and what student behaviour and achievement they expect.'

In a statement that has particular relevance for the nurturance of the human spirit, Steere (1985: 34–35) sees the special contribution of the teacher as confirming the 'deepest thing' which a student has within herself or himself: 'How many men and women can point back to a teacher who saw and believed in them when they neither saw nor believed in this deepest thing in themselves, and can witness to its decisiveness in their own self-discovery and subsequent life quest? The teacher did not put the deepest thing there. It was there already. But he confirmed it.'

Probably the answer to Steere's question is 'Quite a lot'. The Friends' School hopes that its students will be among these.

Conclusion

In a recent article, Rachael Kessler (1999: 50–1) writes of six inter-related yearnings in young people which reflect 'the true nature of spirituality': the search for meaning and purpose, the longing for silence and solitude, the urge for transcendence, the hunger for joy and delight, the drive to create and the need for celebratory initiations. And she goes on to endorse Miller's observation (1996: 5) that '[s]pirituality is nourished, not through formal rituals that students practice in school, but by the *quality of relationship* that is developed between person and world.' This relationship takes the form of 'deep connections' to the self, to other persons or groups, and to nature, one's lineage or a higher power. With respect to the first of these (connecting with the self) Kessler states (51):

> As teachers, we can nourish this connection by giving students time for solitary reflection. Classroom exercises that encourage reflection and expression through writing or art also allow a student access to the inner self while in the midst of other people. Their total engrossment in such creative activities encourages students to discover and express their own feelings, values and beliefs.

Genuine connecting with other persons or groups in a relationship of 'community' is difficult, for, as Palmer states (1999: 11):

> Community emerges when we are willing to share the real concerns of our lives. But in our society, you are reluctant to bring your concerns to me because you fear I am going to try to 'fix' you – and I am reluctant to receive your concerns because I fear I am going to have to 'fix' you! We have no middle ground between invading one

another and ignoring one another, and thus we have no community. But by practicing ground rules that release us from our mutual fears, by teaching us how to live our questions with one another rather than answer them, the gift of community emerges among us – a gift of transformation.

This same thinking is captured in the statement attributed to Lily Walker (quoted by Marilyn McMeniman 1999): 'If you are here to help me, you are wasting your time. But if you come because your liberation is bound up in mine, then let us begin.'

One of my colleagues at Ecolint was Monsieur Dupuy, the teacher of world geography. When a new class came to him, the first thing he would do was to ask the children, each in turn, to show him their countries in the national atlas which they had been asked to bring with them. 'Show me your Holland', he would say to a Dutch boy, and the boy would point proudly to a map of Holland filling up a whole page – and on the opposite page perhaps a map of the US or the USSR filling the same amount of page space. Then he would take the child by the hand and say, 'Now let's go to find Holland on our world map', which extended right over the ceiling and down the four walls. They would search and eventually find Holland – a tiny area high up in a corner of the ceiling. This experience of seeing Holland in a world perspective wasn't meant to imply that Holland was unimportant because of the smallness of its area. The first lesson in world geography was to see one's country in relation to the rest of the world. Since 1949, as the World Commission on Environment and Development (1987: 1) reminds us, we have seen our planet from space for the first time: 'From space, we see a small and fragile ball dominated not by human activity and edifice but by a pattern of clouds, oceans, greenery and soils.' This drives home to us the fact that we are all, indeed, a part of an immense whole, and that an educational system which does not nurture a sense of deep connection with what Paul Davies called 'the miracle of the universe' is failing in one of its prime tasks.

As Hedley Beare said in the Buntine Oration (1987: 24–5):

… we do not really want grey schools that are merely efficient. Rather we need green schools that will take us into our inner temples and inspire us with a sense of awe. We need schools which sponsor contemplation. Nor do we want grey schools that are merely and measurably effective. Rather we need green schools that make us transcend ourselves, presenting us with what we recognise as mythic, memorable and magnificent. We need schools that celebrate the ineffable in ourselves, in others, in the cosmos. Nor do we need grey schools that are merely excellent. Rather we want green schools that focus on, concentrate our vision, that give us the ability to see through things to their deeper beingness.... It is vision ... which drives people on to their highest achievements. And educators must never allow themselves to be diverted from that kind of transcendent purpose.

Both Ecolint and The Friends' School have tried to meet these challenges.

References

Beare, H. 1987. *Shared Meanings About Education: The Economic Paradigm Considered*. The Australian College of Education: Carlton, Victoria.
Campbell, J., McMeniman, M.M. and Baikaloff, N. 1992. *Visions of a Future Australian Society: Towards an Educational Curriculum for 2000 AD and Beyond*. Ministerial Consultative Council on Curriculum: Brisbane.
Capra, F. 1988. *Uncommon Wisdom*. William Collins: London.
Courtney, B. 1989. *The Power of One*. Heinemann: Melbourne.
Davies, P. 1990. *God and the New Physics*. Penguin: London.
Hill, B. 1992. Values education in State schools. *New Horizons in Education*, no. 87.
Kessler, R. 1999. Nourishing students in secular schools. *Educational Leadership*, vol. 56, no. 4.
McMeniman, M.M. 1999. Engaging the Educational Vision: Handing Control to the Imaginative and Empathic Learner. Paper presented at WEF 40th International Conference, Launceston.
Miller, R. 1996. The renewal of education and culture: a multifaceted task. *Great Ideas in Education*, vol. 7, no. 5.
Palmer, P.J. 1999. Evoking the spirit in public education. *Educational Leadership*, vol. 56, no. 4.
Sichel, B. 1988. *Moral Education: Character, Community and Ideals*. Temple University Press: Philadelphia.
Steere, D.V. 1985. *On Confirming Another: Together in Solitude*. Crossroad: New York.
World Commission on Environment and Development. 1987. *Our Common Future*. Oxford University Press: Oxford.

— *Five* —

EDUCATING FOR MORAL RESPONSIBILITY

Brian V. Hill

Was it the good fairy or the wicked fairy who gave us high technology? For those who believe that for every human dilemma or environmental crisis a technological fix will be found, the answer is clearly the good fairy. For those who believe that high technology is a supreme achievement of human hubris, the poisoned chalice that will enable us to destroy ourselves, the answer is equally certainly the bad fairy. But the true answer lies in Reinhold Niebuhr's comment (1941: 160): 'Human history is indeed filled with *endless possibilities*; and the Renaissance saw this more clearly than either Classicism, Catholicism or the Reformation. But it did not recognize that history is filled with endless possibilities of *good and evil*.' This sets the agenda for the education of human beings. While a competent understanding of the world of high technology is not to be neglected, nor is the realm of moral responsibility and concern for the common good. It is a pervasive theme in the present book that human beings must be alerted to the dependence of their humanity on the quality of the moral choices they make on behalf of themselves and others.

The theme has the potential to generate platitudes aplenty, and many writers seem to think that the mere act of pronouncing what is good will make it so. But 'there's many a slip twixt the cup and the lip'. Even Socrates found this a problem. He expressed puzzlement that virtuous people sometimes have vicious children. Nevertheless, he was still prepared to assert that those who *knew* the good would by that fact be inclined to *do* it. By contrast, philosopher William Frankena (1958: 300–13), in an important article published over forty years ago, discounted this easy confidence in rationality. And, of course, he was not the first to do so. A Christian Jew called Paul, two millennia earlier, testified to the fact that often, though he knew what he ought to do, he failed to do it (*The Bible: New International Version* 1973).

Frankena supported his contention by arguing that there are two distinct tasks in moral education: one, to develop *knowledge* of the good and the right, which he called Moral Education X (MEX), and the other, to ensure that children's *conduct* conformed to this knowledge, which he called Moral Education Y (MEY). They are two different tasks, as two people working within Lawrence Kohlberg's cognitive-developmental paradigm ruefully discovered. At a conference in Ottawa, Oliver and Bane (1971: 260) expressed dismay that 'although students sometimes become very excited about the issues raised by the cases, they seldom seem to take the issues seriously in a personal sense'. Students might discuss issues of justice with great skill and insight in the classroom, but it did not affect their playground morality. Bullies continued unashamedly to bully, and so on. (It reminded me of the story of a foul-mouthed bully in one school, who swaggered up to the bulletin board with his uncouth hangers-on, and suddenly exclaimed in surprise: 'Hey, you guys, I've just won the bloody ethics prize!' Which surely suggests a high score for MEX and a minus score for MEY!) Oliver and Bane speculated that their cognitive approach in the classroom might profit from the parallel involvement of students in significant happenings, such as religious celebrations and voluntary camping.

The gap between MEX and MEY is one reason why so many people are sceptical about moral education through schooling. And there are other reasons as well. What I want to do first in this chapter is to address this and some other objections to moral education, attempting to show that the problems they pose are not insuperable. Second, I want to identify some weighty reasons why we must make a case *for* moral education. Third, I will attempt to suggest some guidelines which will help us to achieve the goal of moral education, assuming that the goal in question includes the development in our students of both a sense of moral responsibility for their own actions and a concern for the common good.

The Case *against* Moral Education

For some time it has been unfashionable to talk about moral education. The emphasis has tended to be on intellectual education, supported by extensive and illuminating research into cognitive development. More recently, an earthier emphasis has entered educational discourse, stressing the performative skills necessary to equip students for effective participation in the work-forces of nations involved in economic re-structuring. Admittedly, there has also been some important research into attitudinal change, but it has been directed mostly towards understanding the *development* of attitudes, rather than nominating those attitudes which we wish to modify through education. When that question is raised, educational theorists run for cover. Equally, administrators in State systems of education have been reluctant to commit the curriculum to the promotion of particular attitudes and values, especially in the religious, moral and political realms, for fear of showing partisanship towards particular belief systems. Both turn a blind eye to the fact that commitments to intellectual and/or industrial outcomes are just as value laden.

There are, of course, some philosophical objections to moral education which appear to endorse such moves. These can be depicted by simulating a conversation between Premier Politic, Mrs Pluralist and Dr Analytic.

Premier Politic is an Australian in his fifties (bearing no resemblance whatever, of course, to any contemporary premier!). He belongs to the old school and believes that the only way to protect State schools from the charge of indoctrination is to insist that such schools maintain total neutrality towards value issues. In particular, areas of controversy such as religion, morality and politics are altogether off limits. Let the schools concentrate on teaching basic skills of literacy and numeracy, the academic disciplines and vocational skills (or, at least, pre-vocational skills).

Mrs Pluralist, an articulate recent migrant, objects that Premier Politic is far from maintaining a neutral stance. His ideas, she says, are peculiarly Western and tacitly endorse the domination of Anglo-Saxon values. She argues for a more consciously *multicultural* curriculum, to which Premier Politic replies irascibly: 'And you'll be the first person to complain if your children come home reporting that they've been taught about other faiths and questioning yours. Anyway, we don't want our State schools to promote division; we want them to promote a common allegiance to our nation.'

Mrs Pluralist replies, 'Well, there's nothing neutral about that suggestion, is there, any more than there was in your earlier defence of a very academic curriculum. I'm glad you brought it into the open. We all need to be upfront about the values we believe in. And I agree that we should encourage a sense of common citizenship. But I also think we should promote cultural diversity.'

Dr Analytic, a tense junior academic suffering from postmodernitis, can contain himself no longer. 'What you both don't realise', he says, 'is that whether you're teaching one dominant belief system or several, you're using the school to indoctrinate instead of educate. The focus of what we do at school should be the development of critical thinking. Equip students with the mental skills to make up their own minds; to think, not just to conform.'

'Oh, yes', interrupts Premier Politic crossly, 'turn them into critics and rebels. After all, who wants loyal citizens!'

'Loyal to what?' asks Dr Analytic sharply. 'We can't claim any longer that one view of life is right and the rest wrong. We've got to respect people's right to construct their own meaning, provided they don't infringe on someone else's right to do the same. The school's task is to teach them to think, not to dictate their values.'

Mrs Pluralist looks perplexed: 'Yes, but don't you need something to think *about* as well? And some encouragement to adopt *worthy* attitudes and values? You can have loyal critics, surely?'

Dr Analytic shakes his head as though he's dealing with a slow child. 'Who decides what's "worthy"? We all have different mental maps. The only legitimate response is to live and let live.'

'That's a value-loaded point of view, too', says Mrs Pluralist, 'and again, I'm actually happy to agree with it as far as it goes, but I also want to encourage dialogue and negotiation between groups to make this a better society.'

'Better?' mutters Dr Analytic, but Premier Politic has the floor: 'Exactly. We want a democracy based on a common way of life, not ethnic enclaves all over the place. If you people are going to come *here*, you should be prepared to accept our values.'

Mrs Pluralist sighs and offers them both a cup of tea. On that point, at least, she encounters no disagreement.

* * * *

From the foregoing, we may distill three common criticisms of attempts to validate intentional moral education.

1. One says that the only options are neutralism or indoctrination, and since indoctrination is antipathetic to education, value neutrality is therefore the only viable option for schools.
2. A second claims that pluralism and post-modern relativism have carried us beyond the possibility of consensus on what values to promote.
3. A third doubts whether, even if the previous objections could be overcome, education would be able to bridge the gap between knowing the good and doing it.

Additional deterrents of a more practical kind include the increasing tendency to blame schools for all the ills of our society, and the equally accelerating inclination of our citizens to go to litigation if anything does not please them. Teachers, in particular, seem to have no friends, so, it is suggested by some, they had better just keep their heads down and teach facts and skills.

Can the force of such arguments be blunted?

Is neutralism really the only educational option?

First, let us grant that, in modern educational usage, 'indoctrination' is a term of disapproval applied to teaching which tries to fix certain beliefs and values in the learner without allowing critical inspection and choice with respect to them. Is there any possibility of charting a course between the Scylla of neutralism and the Charybdis of indoctrination? I have argued elsewhere (Hill 1981: 59–70) that the solution is to adopt a dual policy of transmitting the heritage while at the same time developing the skills of values analysis and critical evaluation. It's a both-and. We can agree on the need to inform students of the beliefs and values significant in their culture, on condition that we also equip them with the capacity to interrogate those sources and justify the values they themselves choose to adopt. It is the second condition that is the crucial safeguard against indoctrination, aiming, as it does, to liberate rather than to cloister.

An interesting example of these principles being put into practice may be seen in the Year 12 project report once submitted by a student in New South Wales. The daughter of recent Thai migrants, she elected to develop a comparison of her life story with that of a cousin of the same age still living in Thailand (Hudson 1993). Here was an opportunity to both affirm and examine the beliefs and values in her own upbringing, along with the influences brought to bear upon her in a new culture. The 'Tale of Two Cousins' was a striking example of values education in the best sense.

Is consensus really an impossible goal?

It is argued that societies are on the road to pluralism of values rather than convergence. Added to this fact is the post-modern sensitivity to the oppressive dominant narratives through which ruling elites are alleged to have controlled societies in the past. In these circumstances, the answer to the above question lies in a double-barrelled policy of being willing to let all voices be heard, while at the same time working for agreement on a minimum charter of individual rights and community goods. The big gamble here is whether the common ground identified by such a dialogue will be robust enough to sustain democratic life at a high level. Many years ago, Alfred Whitehead (1959: 107) said presciently: 'We are at the threshold of a democratic age, and it remains to be determined whether the equality of [humanity] is to be realised on a high level or a low level.' It would be a salutary exercise to speculate on what he would think of the global society that is now evolving. Would he consider the consumer society a realisation of human hopes at a *high* level? Would he perceive the competitive bottom line of economic rationalism to be a secure base for the human rights embodied in the democratic ideal?

Some feel it is too late to hope that anything but the most superficial agreement can be reached between the differing interests of the ethnic and other sub-cultures which have proliferated in modern societies, let alone the multinational monopolies which are today turning national governments into mere tenderers for economic preference. This is an empirical question, and I will suggest later that there are some encouraging signs that, in fact, it *can* be done.

Is moral conduct really beyond the teacher's reach?

It is not a foregone conclusion that just because it is a difficult task, we must give up the attempt to persuade students to engage in behaviour that is morally responsible and concerned for the common good. It is undoubtedly difficult, but it is manifestly achieved in many cases, and the challenge for educators is to be wiser about the many fronts on which we need to work. We have been too prone to believe that the school and classroom can do the whole job. The research evidence is against us. Elsewhere (Hill 1990: 22), I have argued that schools which seek to foster attitudes, beliefs and values appear to succeed only when they are broadly reflecting and endorsing the home background and social class of their students. Attempts to change students' values in directions contrary to these influences generally seem to make little difference.

But this is not to say that the school has no part to play at all. It is well situated to service a substantial agenda:

- informing students of the worlds of value which characterise the pluralistic society;
- developing the tools of analysis and empathy that will enable students to process those data and reconcile them with their own backgrounds; and
- encouraging the kinds of interaction that make for a caring and convivial society.

To adopt a façade of neutrality is to betray this achievable mandate. At the same time, the school has to accept that it is only one of several partners in the project of values education. The virtues of schooling have been oversold in current educational theory. As a highly stylised social institution, it is significantly limited in what it can achieve, or ought even try to achieve, in the area of value change. Too often, professional snobbery prevents teachers from seeing that they *must* draw parents into the process, even if it obliges them to attempt a certain amount of *parent* education as well. An eminent New Zealand Director-General of Education once said (Renwick 1977: 12):

More than any other professional group I can think of except the clergy and social workers, teachers must develop their professionalism not as something that widens the gulf between themselves and other members of society but as something capable of closing it. A tall order this for an occupational group which, for long enough, has aspired to the kind of professionalism exemplified by doctors and lawyers – one derived from the mystique of esoteric knowledge known only to the chosen few.

In principle, parents are the people who know the individual child best, have legitimate aspirations for their children's moral education and need to be persuaded that the school's value charter will not subvert their efforts in this direction but complement them. But like schools, parents, too, to a significant extent, exercise *compulsion* over the child. A third partner is needed – one dedicated to encouraging *voluntary* commitment through example and persuasion rather than securing conformity through rule and social control. This is the role which, in modern societies, has increasingly been played by voluntary youth services. In the guided youth group, leaders have little formal power, but by the same token they have great influence. Representing the value commitments for which their group stands – whether they relate to stamp collecting, adventure camping, religious allegiance or whatever – they can and must rely only on open persuasion.

Equally openly, however, they may recommend the values that they themselves believe in, and young people may 'try them on', without risk of reprisal if they then choose not to adopt them. Paradoxically, it is usually in such voluntary contexts that personal responsibility and commitment to worthy values come to full flower. Ideally, the partnership of home, school and voluntary group can fulfil the requirements of both MEX and MEY. If any one of the three is in default, then all else is remedial education.

There are, of course, other influences which affect, for good or ill, the moral education of the young person. We have mentioned wider social and cultural influences, many of which need to be resisted because of their exploitative intent. On the other side of the ledger, we may cite educational media and democratic political institutions, both of which at their best aim to liberate rather than enslave. In short, granted that the task of moving beyond MEX to MEY is daunting, it is not in principle unachievable, and there is evidence that many agencies do in fact achieve it. Our job is to strengthen the partnership amongst those agencies that are benevolent in intent.

The Case *for* Moral Education

This is an appropriate point at which to turn the coin over and to recognise that there are powerful reasons for giving the *highest priority* to moral education.

Values Indoctrination by Default

We noted that many people have felt apprehensive about bringing the teaching of values into the formal curriculum. At the same time, however, by default, some very powerful values are being thrust upon our children from outside sources, filling the values vacuum with consumerist longings. Material goods are marketed with the aid of irrelevant sexual innuendoes, luxuries are touted as necessities, and TV programmers hope by titillation and violence to keep customers glued to the segments paid for by their commercial clients.

How can anyone claim that society will find its own level, when well-financed profiteers have such powerful tools of manipulation at their disposal? We need both to develop in children a critical *resistance* to such lures and to show them that there are better values for living than those valorised by the commercial world. The case *for* moral education begins here. Neutrality is a myth. Even if we were to succeed in bleaching our educational services of all explicit reference to values, the surrounding society has no such qualms. Sectarian groups, rapacious media barons and convinced racists are all in the business of exploiting the young, trading on youthful inexperience and vulnerability to fulfil their own objectives.

Delinquent Parents

Faced with such competition, many parents are giving up on moral education, some because they themselves are morally perplexed, and some, apparently, because they don't even care. Analysts of what Americans call 'Generation X' are saying that one of the strongest features of this cohort is a profound disillusionment with an adult generation which has left them to bring themselves up while it pursues its own indulgences (Rushkoff 1997).

So who is left? Where can we find agencies whose first priority is the development of young people? As I suggested earlier, the other two primary agencies are schools and voluntary youth organisations. In principle, they are our best hope, but in practice, they often fall short. School systems in most countries today are under great pressure to put targets of national productivity before individual needs, while voluntary groups sometimes turn out to be disguised recruiting depots for ideological causes. But at least such agencies are expected to put their aims upfront, and we can hold them accountable for the development of discerning young people capable of exercising moral responsibility and of working for the common good.

Cultural Fragmentation

Other imperatives, also global in their scope, oblige us to make the attempt. Pluralism – that is, the diversity of world-views and value stances which are present in any modernising society today – while it may make it harder to achieve consensus on what should be done, makes it all the more urgent that we try. The explosive effects of conflict between religious and ethnic enclaves are already visible in many countries. Furthermore, in the light of our opening comment about the need to marry technological and moral considerations, reconciliation is both an economic *and* a moral task.

Environmental Crisis

Added to this, a relatively new moral concern has come to the fore. Our global habitat is under threat. The last decade has seen an enormous increase in public consciousness of the degree to which our planet is imperilled by pollution, deforestation and the extinction of species. Economic selfishness is rampant. Some see our salvation in technological innovation but, as we noted at the beginning, technology is morally ambivalent, and just as likely to be the destroyer as the saviour. What's *also* needed is the moral will to apply technology in the interests of economic policies that renew and sustain the environment. Unfortunately, recent educational policies have been running strongly towards vocational and technical competencies geared primarily to economic productivity *per se,* and we urgently need to explore ways of bringing moral and values education to the fore.

An interesting exercise in building bridges between technological and moral discourse was provided at the 1999 WEF Conference in Launceston by Steve Keirl, a lecturer in the University of South Australia. Laying out on the floor dozens of variations on the humble dishwashing mop, he demonstrated how many value issues could be raised in the course of discussing the technology it represented, ranging from form and function in design, to conspicuous consumption, gender roles in the home, economic distribution and so on. The implications for teaching in the curriculum area of Technology are wide-ranging.

Such, then, are some of the factors that oblige us to take moral education seriously. And they make teachers and youth workers our front-line troops. The tasks of MEX and MEY are huge, but some guidelines can help us get started.

Guidelines to Moral Education

The proof of the pudding depends in part on our being able to operationalise the worthy sentiments that are often expressed in this connection, sentiments which otherwise may be no more than stirring but sterile rhetoric. Five suggestions are made below for improving our performance in moral and values education.

Developing a Discourse

First, we need to develop a discourse which will enable us to talk about values in their own right, and not just as social facts wholly accounted for by social-scientific description. That may seem a superfluous suggestion, given that in our day-to-day living we talk about values all the time, albeit, it should be noted, in prescriptive ways. There is also much confusion and emotion in ordinary usage. Take, for example, the idea of people needing to 'justify' their values. In the study of ethics, the justification of values is a very systematic pursuit, but in everyday usage the idea of justification tends to be debased in either of two ways. First, it may be interpreted as 'self-justification', as when I use whatever persuasive means I can to defend my actions, whether good or bad. Second, many people do not even think you *can* justify values, because they believe that values are simply the expression of arbitrary subjective wants.

Or take the word 'values' itself. Are we referring to cognitive or emotional states? Are values the same as wants? Are all values on the same level, or do 'higher' values override instrumental values? What counts as truth in the ethical domain?

The 'values clarification' movement of the 1970s (Raths, Harmin and Simon 1978) performed a useful function in showing how discourse and negotiation skills can be developed in a classroom setting. Many good teaching materials emanated from this movement. But it was also beholden to an emotive theory of ethics which devalued rational justification. I have argued elsewhere (Hill 1994: 50) that justification is a necessary intermediate step between clarification and interpersonal negotiation.

In this regard, useful strategies were suggested at the 1999 WEF Conference by Val Catchpoole, who had put to good use her experience in the production of children's television. She compiled a kit utilising several excerpts from stories presented on the Australian Broadcasting Corporation network. These were woven into lessons posing questions about the moral intentions and consequences illustrated by these episodes. Explaining her approach, Catchpoole was at pains to defend the use of stories designed primarily to entertain, rather than ones written with deliberate didactic intent.

Negotiating Core Values

Second, it is important to extend the practice of negotiating on core values. I wrote earlier of the scepticism with which many people view such a recommendation today, believing that there is no longer any real possibility of achieving a workable consensus. But the alternative is social disintegration. And I believe that there are many signs that it *is* actually possible to achieve a useful level of agreement. For example, the fiftieth birthday of the Universal Declaration of Human Rights has just been celebrated. No doubt many nations are still giving lip service to the Universal Declaration while honouring it in the breach, but it has nevertheless been a very useful court of appeal when humanitarians have sought ways to shine the spotlight on situations in which human rights are being seriously abused. And it provides a valuable agenda for educating children in values discourse, and alerting them to some of the humane values that have gained wide support. In the second chapter of this book, Colin N. Power provides useful confirmation that the Universal Declaration, and many of the policies of

UNESCO, have made far more headway than the public is generally aware of. Again, consider the Declaration framed by the Parliament of the World's Religions convened in Chicago in 1993 and published under the title *A Global Ethic* (Kung and Kuschel 1993). As the editors wisely say in the preface: 'A global ethic does not reduce the religions to an ethical minimalism but represents *the minimum of what the religions of the world already have in common now in the ethical sphere*' (8, their italics).

A practical suggestion for initiating a discussion of rights made by British authors Pike and Selby (quoted in Lemin *et al.* 1994: 149) involves a 'rights balloon'. Students are to imagine that they are in a leaking hot-air balloon, along with nine human rights weighing three kilos each. To stay aloft they must progressively jettison the rights they value least, justifying their choices. The nine rights are:

> The right to vote
> The right to meet freely with others of my choice
> The right to travel freely in my neighbourhood, State
>   and country
> The right to hold any job for which I am qualified
> The right to be educated to the extent of my desire
>   and ability
> The right to marry the person of my choice
> The right to a fair trial
> The right to hold political views of my choice
> The right to hold religious views of my choice

The suggestion is that individually or in pairs students compile their own initial lists, and then defend their priorities in wider discussion. In order to get beyond mere clarification to considerations of what are traditionally perceived as common goods, it would be important to follow up this kind of lesson with studies of global and communal value charters.

For example, on a local level, Chapter 3 describes the study carried out by Campbell, McMeniman and Baikaloff (1992) which generated a 'workable' consensus on national goals and provided the conceptual framework of this present volume. Again, in the present author's home State of Western Australia, a consortium was brought together in the non-State school sector in 1994 to evaluate the place of values education in a so-called National Curriculum that had just been published. The review led to two significant outcomes. One was an attempt to explore the possibilities of consensus amongst several religious communities operating schools in the private sector. Somewhat to everyone's surprise, a substantial Agreed Minimum Values Framework emerged from this exercise (WA Values Review Project 1995), from which practical guidelines for classroom teachers have since been developed and taken up by many teachers. In a climate of constant curriculum revision which has left teachers feeling jaded and cynical about each new incursion on their time, it has been exhilarating to have so many teachers welcome these initiatives as helpful and affirming. The other outcome was the adoption in 1998 of a large part of that same Values Framework by a Government Curriculum Council, legislating for both State and non-State schools (Curriculum Council of Western Australia 1998). It constitutes an interesting case-study, which Tom Wallace (1999) has recently described.

It was examples such as these that encouraged me to urge that we 'extend the practice of negotiating on core values'. The guideline was phrased in this way to drive home the point that ideally the compilation of a values charter is never set once and for all, but is an ongoing exercise which improves with practice, and is carried out in all sorts of settings. Schools, for example, which are pluralistic communities in their own right, need to extend the practice, drawing all the stakeholders into an ongoing dialogue – one which includes students, parents, staff and members of the wider community. If a school keeps its values charter under continuous review in this way, teachers in the classroom will gain confidence that their efforts to venture into this terrain, in the spirit of the charter, are likely to be supported. In addition, the educational benefits for students are potentially huge, especially when each successive cohort is encouraged, through participation in such a review, to make the charter they inherited their own.

Rehabilitating the Common Good

The third guideline amplifies the second. One may ask: What kinds of values ought we to spell out in a democratic charter for a school? Currently a tide is flowing in Australia towards the devolution of management responsibility to local schools. Each school is being expected to develop a policy statement of its own. However, such statements are mainly directed to identifying management outcomes of a technical kind, and there is reason to believe that the move is a ploy to disguise a government push towards privatisation and the contraction of public funding. Nevertheless, it provides an opportunity to pitch the debate at a higher level.

What I am arguing for is the need to include the identification of agreed values. And these in turn need to be of two kinds: rights and goals. The idea of liberal democracy as it has developed in the West has focused mainly on the former. We know what we want to *protect* (rights) but we are uncertain what we ought to *promote* (goals). Rights protect individual freedom, but they do not necessarily promote mutual co-operation and common goods. Indeed, the term 'common good', even where it has not gone out of fashion, tends to be defined in negative or defensive terms. The deficiency is most clearly felt in education, because of its concern with human development. In lieu of a positive vision of personal and community life, educational outcomes tend to be spelled out in pragmatic terms which, as noted previously, incline currently to emphasise competencies that will enhance the nation's international competitiveness, at the expense of more directly humane objectives. The Western Australian values review produced a much wider mandate than this.

Celebrating Diversity

The fourth guideline is the other side of the coin, echoing the balance being sought by Mrs Pluralist in the imagined conversation at the beginning of the chapter. It represents a commitment to affirming individuals whatever their cultural backgrounds, which is the 'rights' side of the ledger, whilst at the same time encouraging the diverse expressions of cultural creativity they represent, which contributes to the 'goals' side. Premier Politic feared that this would encourage division, but ignoring or suppressing these expressions of cultural diversity is even more likely to do just that. By contrast, there is much to be gained from transcending the parochialism and fear of the other fostered by discriminatory social practices. Furthermore, in the school context, a robust endorsement of multiculturalism has the potential to enrich learning enormously. Some educationists, if they do not actually deplore it, regard multicultural diversity in the school as a problem to be overcome, but rather it is an opportunity to be seized.

The Pullenvale Environmental Education Centre in Queensland (Tooth 1993) provides an interesting example of how empathy, without which cognitive gain will never be translated into moral will, may be enhanced. Students visiting the centre on school trips are caught up in a 'story thread', beginning with the discovery of an old coded message stick calling for help. Fragments of a diary written in 1860 by a fictional boy called Tom describe his friendship with the Aboriginal boy Jagara, and the racial tensions and oppressions of the time. Drawn back to the present, the students meet two Aboriginal friends who describe how their grandmothers were institutionalised in children's homes, and discussions raise many issues of historical accuracy, respect for each other's cultures and the preservation of environmental heritage.

Diversity is not the same as deviancy. There are those who, in the name of diversity, would like to remove all restraints on human behaviour. Like Dr Analytic, they have a kind of free market view of values. Not only is this a very individualistic approach to the issue, it also leaves the door open to forms of psychic assault and self-abuse from which the community, and especially the young and weak, have a right to be protected. The safeguard here is the negotiated common good of the previous guideline. By implication, this will include setting limits which will, to that extent, constitute an agreed definition of what is evil – at least in a communal sense. And these limits will need to be policed.

Educating Better People

The final guideline recommends that we aim quite consciously to help learners develop into better people, resisting the timidity which falls back on merely technical goals and economic criteria. Stated at the beginning of this chapter, this proposition would have sounded platitudinous, but I hope that my attempts to spell out what such ideas imply in practice has given both goals more body, and this in two ways. First, a case has been made for values education, directed towards a negotiated common good. The vision I have tried to justify carries us, in Whitehead's words, towards a democracy at a high level. A 'better world' will not come about without better people trying to make it so. Let it be said yet again that the answer does not lie solely with unbridled technology or research, but with a sharing of moral vision. Second, we need bold educational policies which carry the individual from the mere getting of knowledge to the achievement of critical autonomy, and from this to a critical loyalty to humane personal and communal values. Ways have been foreshadowed in which this agenda can be more specifically spelled out and achieved, and there is a burgeoning literature of practical suggestions, additional examples of which I have incorporated in the references to this chapter (Beck, Crittenden and Sullivan 1971; Brady 1978; Dufty 1970; Fraenkel 1958; Hersh, Miller and Fielding 1980; Hill 1991; Leverenz and Oliver 1992; Lipman *et al.* 1980; N.P.D.P. Values Review Project 1997; Oliver and Shaver 1966; Starratt 1994; Stradling *et al.* 1984; *The Values We Teach* 1991; Wringe 1984). Hopefully, the chapter has helped to demonstrate that both MEX and MEY are tenable objectives, even in pluralistic societies.

References

Beck, C., Crittenden, B.S. and Sullivan, E.V. (eds.). 1971. *Moral Education: Interdisciplinary Approaches*. Newman Press: New York.
Bible: New International Version, The. 1973. Zondervan: Grand Rapids, Mich.
Brady, L. 1978. *Feel, Value, Act: Learning about Value Theory and Practice*. Prentice-Hall: Sydney.
Campbell, J., McMeniman, M.M. and Baikaloff, N. 1992. *Visions of a Future Australian Society: Towards an Educational Curriculum for 2000 AD and Beyond*. Ministerial Consultative Council on Curriculum: Brisbane.
Curriculum Council of Western Australia. 1998. *Curriculum Framework: For Kindergarten to Year 12 Education in Western Australia*. Curriculum Council of Western Australia: Perth.
Dufty, D.J. 1970. *Teaching about Society*. Rigby: Adelaide.
Fraenkel, J.R. 1958. *Helping Students Think and Value*. 2nd edn. Prentice-Hall: Englewood Cliffs, NJ.
Frankena, W.K. 1958. Toward a philosophy of moral education. *Harvard Educational Review*, vol. 28.
Hersh, R.H., Miller, J.P. and Fielding, J.D. 1980. *Models of Moral Education: An Appraisal*. Longman: New York.
Hill, B.V. 1981. 'Education for commitment': a logical contradiction? *Journal of Educational Thought*, vol. 15.
———. 1990. *That They May Learn*. Patemoster Press: Exeter.
———. 1991. *Values Education in Australian Schools*. ACER: Melbourne.
———. 1994. *Teaching Secondary Social Studies in a Multicultural Society*. Longman Cheshire: Melbourne.
Hudson, Anne, personal communication, 1993; reported in more detail in Hill, 1994 (72).

78 | *Brian V. Hill*

Kung, H., and Kuschel, Karl-Josef (eds.). 1993. *A Global Ethic: The Declaration of the Parliament of the World's Religions*. SCM: London.

Lemin, M., *et al.* (eds.). 1994. *Values Processes for Classroom Teachers*. ACER: Melbourne.

Leverenz, P., and Oliver, G. 1992. *Issues in Society*. Science Press: Marrickville, NSW.

Lipman, M., *et al.* 1980. *Philosophy in the Classroom*. 2nd edn. Temple University Press: Philadelphia.

Niebuhr, R. 1941. *The Nature and Destiny of Man*. Vol 1. *Human Nature: A Christian Interpretation*. Nisbet and Co., London.

N.P.D.P. Values Review Project. 1997. *Classroom Curriculum Package and School Planning Curriculum Package*. National Professional Development Programme: Perth.

Oliver, D.W., and Bane, M.J. 1971. Moral education: is reasoning enough? In C. Beck, B.S. Crittenden and E.V. Sullivan (eds.). *Moral Education: Interdisciplinary Approaches*. Newman Press: New York.

Oliver, D.W., and Shaver, J.P. 1966. *Teaching Public Issues in the High School*. Houghton Mifflin: Boston.

Raths, L.E., Harmin, M. and Simon, S.B. 1978. *Values and Teaching: Working with Values in the Classroom*. 2nd edn. C.E. Merrill: Chicago.

Renwick, W.L. 1977. Leopards with Changing Spots. Paper presented to the Fourth National Conference of the Australian Council for Educational Administration, Brisbane.

Rushkoff, D. 1997. *Children of Chaos: Surviving the End of the World as We Know It*. Harper Collins: London.

Starratt, R.J. 1994. *Building an Ethical School*. Falmer: London.

Stradling, R., *et al.* 1984. *Teaching Controversial Issues*. Edward Arnold: London.

Tooth, R. 1993. *The Pullenvale Storythread Model*. Queensland Department of Education: Brisbane.

Values We Teach, The. 1991. Department of School Education: NSW, Sydney.

Wallace, T. 1999. Mainstreaming values in schooling in Western Australia. *Journal of Christian Education*, vol. 72, no. 1.

WA Values Review Project. 1995. *Minimum Values Framework*. National Professional Development Programme Values Review Project: Perth.

Whitehead, A.N. 1959. *Aims of Education and Other Essays*. Ernest Benn: London.

Wringe, C. 1984. *Democracy, Schooling and Political Education*. Allen and Unwin: London.

Six

EDUCATING FOR UNITY THROUGH DIVERSITY OF KNOWING

A Systemic Perspective

Richard J. Bawden

Introduction

It is a cruel irony with respect to the foundational principles of both UNESCO and WEF that, even as this chapter is being written (May 1999), bombs are again falling in Europe. Once more there are those who continue to flout the call for 'peace in our time', who continue to fail to respect cultural and ethnic differences. And it is perhaps no surprise that the current tragedy is being played out within the Balkans, for 'balkanisation' has become a virtual synonym for differentiation and the compartmentalisation of distinctions, standing in direct contrast to the kind of synthesis sought through a belief in the value of 'unity through diversity'.

It is not my intention here to dwell long on the dynamics of the terrible conflict in Yugoslavia, or to focus on the dozen or more examples of the vicious, ethnically and religiously based hostilities that are in full expression in various countries somewhere on almost every continent at the moment. That said, there are some profoundly disturbing elements about the current situation that are illustrating the apparent inadequacy of education over the years to change situations where particular views of the world – and the specific beliefs and value positions that they reflect – continue to colonise the minds of 'men'. Whether it be repulsive racial and religious repression, on the one hand, or the brutal reliance on techno-scientific warfare in response, on the other, the crisis in the Balkans does little to inspire confidence in the power of the pen to still the sword.

Yet, surely, it is the hope of us all that education will win through and that, through its influence, the common good will come to prevail across the globe. I want here to explore the notion that, just as, in the words of UNESCO's Constitution, 'it is in the minds of men [*sic*] that the defences of peace must be constructed', so, too, must it be in the minds of individuals that unity in diversity is to be nurtured.

Of particular relevance here will be a set of ideas drawn from so-called systems theories and philosophies, which hold that coherent unities (called systems) have particular properties precisely because of the interactions among their diverse parts. Indeed, whole systems need requisite levels of diversity in order to allow them to be different from the sums of their parts, and to retain their coherence in the face of the diverse challenges from the environments in which they must operate. Unity is possible only through diversity.

The submission here is that contemporary education is almost universally characterised by inadequate levels of diversity itself. It is, therefore, failing even to understand, let alone encourage, the phenomenon in any other human domain. For the design of more robust learning systems there is considerable empathy with the claim of Robert Hutchins (1976) that '[c]ivilization can be saved only by a moral, intellectual and spiritual revolution to match the scientific, technological and economic revolution in which we are living. If education can contribute to that then it offers a real hope of salvation to suffering humanity everywhere. If it cannot, or will not … then it is irrelevant, and its fate is immaterial.' I am among those who seek to contribute to Hutchins's revolution, by helping to cultivate 'unity in learning' through the appreciation and accommodation of the inherent diversity in different moral, intellectual and spiritual paradigms.

Diverse Ways of Knowing

Amending a submission by Reason and Heron (1986) in only one significant respect, let me start with the statement that it is useful to consider four different ways by which we humans can come to know anything. Each way involves us in different processes of knowing and each results in different forms of knowledge. For the moment, and in apparent contradiction to my theme, I want to argue for the distinctions between them – presenting them as if each was quite different and unrelated to the others. This is a position that I will later change, but for the moment it is convenient to illustrate diversity before arguing the case for unity. It is very difficult to build a case in support of the whole if one has no feel for the nature of the parts that compose it, or appreciation of the challenges inherent in their synthesis.

In the first process of knowing, I can gain *propositional* knowledge. I acquire propositions essentially by being told through some medium or another – through communicating face to face, through reading a book or through accessing the World Wide Web. Propositional knowing is concerned with knowing for its own sake. This kind of knowledge is validated either through direct reference to the source from which it was gained, or through the use of a particular logic which supports its construction. My acquired knowledge of scientific propositions can, for instance, be assessed by someone who taught me science in the first place, or I can evaluate it within a theoretical framework appropriate to the logic of the particular discipline that I am studying. Alternatively, I can test it empirically. To test the idea of gravity, for instance, I can let drop a host of different things from my grasp to evaluate the predictability of their descent.

The ability to carry out more sophisticated experiments, however, relies on a second category of knowing concerned with doing. *Practical* knowledge is know-how. It is acquired essentially by being shown, and it is validated in similar fashion. If I want to claim that I know how to ride a bicycle, for instance, you will remain unconvinced until such time as you see me actually riding one. Practical knowledge is all too often referred to as skill and demeaned as a 'lower order' of human capability. In the present context, however, there is no difference in quality whatsoever between propositional and practical knowledge. The difference lies in the way each form of knowledge is acquired and how it is validated.

As a third way of knowing, I can acquire knowledge from my own experiences. *Experiential* knowledge is formally defined as that which is created through the transformation of personal experience. It occurs as the outcome of my attempts to make sense out of what is happening directly to me in my interactions with the world about me and with others in it. I validate that which I have come to know experientially through self-evaluation. Just as experiential knowledge is created rather than acquired, so too must the mechanisms that are used in its validation be created. In other words, the process of validation is contextual. It's a type of process of familiarisation. I come to know certain people, for instance, through 'experiencing' them in some way or another, and I know that I know them because I can recognise them in a crowd and be recognised by them in turn. The same can be said for becoming familiar with particular places, or with any other circumstance or event that can be experienced in the concrete. The essential point to be emphasised here is that experiential knowing involves all of me in the process – not just my mind or my hands, but my whole being. It is thus knowing for being. I can come to know (propositionally) the theory of music, just as I can come to know (practically) how to play music on an appropriate instrument. But I can come to know what it is like to be a musician only through the experience of becoming one. And by the phrase 'coming to know', I refer, of course, to the process we call learning.

Clearly, experiential learning provides both a vital context and framework for the synthesis of both propositional and practical learning. Experiential learning leads to personal transformation or adaptation, as David Kolb (1984) would have it, and combines, as a process, 'finding out' activities with those for 'taking action'. In the process of trying to make sense out of something in one's environment, it pays to know propositions that are of relevance to the circumstance. Equally, when trying to do something about adapting to that particular circumstance, there are signal advantages in having a host of appropriate practical knowledge. The interrelationships among the three forms of knowing and learning mentioned so far thus become increasingly evident – with advantages clearly lying in unity through their diversity.

But, as Hutchins's words remind us, there must be very much more to all of this than has been articulated thus far. Propositional, practical and experiential learning can all contribute to the way we reason our way through life – helping us to know what it is that intellectually we *can* or *could* do next – but they are of limited value in helping us know what it is that, morally or spiritually, we *should* do next.

It is in accommodating this latter domain that I digress somewhat from the position originally proposed by Reason and Heron, although I must emphasise that both authors themselves embrace, in a number of ways, that which I am about to describe. Wilber (1997) is another who has developed similar themes. The uniqueness of that which follows with respect to what I am calling *inspirational* knowing lies, firstly, in the manner through which the ideas were created, that is, in tragic circumstances, and, secondly, in their deliberate location within a critical systemic perspective.

My awakening awareness of inspirational knowing and learning as a fourth form of knowledge came from my wife Diane, who in January 1994 was diagnosed with inoperable cancer in the liver. She was to die eighteen months later. Through that period she literally learned how to die, drawing not primarily on propositional, practical or experiential knowledge from 'without', but on insights that came from 'within'. She seemed to possess an intrinsic knowledge which was manifested in the peace, grace, dignity, courage and explicit love that characterised her behaviour throughout her illness, right up to her death. Not a religious person, Diane learned to access and express a profound spirituality.

It was from her, and through the contemplative and essentially meditative processes that she followed to reach, accept and apply those innate insights to give meaning to herself throughout those months, that I learned how to do the same. Through her, I learned not only how to learn inspirationally, but also how to integrate the inspirational outcomes with knowledge derived through the other three domains that I have outlined briefly above. I have learned how to create what I now see as *meaning* that I can use to inform my actions. Where once I relied on thoughtful action, I now do all that I can to make my actions meaningful. It is to my inspirational domain that I now refer as I seek answers to the *should* questions. It is within those deeply embedded insights that I feel moral and ethical guidance can be found: not as inviolate objective tenets, but as insights that help me make meaning out of the concepts and thoughts that I derive experientially, or acquire propositionally. And it is to the inspirational learning process that I must return when I seek validation of my meaningful actions; I can learn how I know what I should do next only from the original source of the inspiration.

It is inspirational learning that allows access to the majority of the values that we hold: those assumptions about what is good and what is evil, what is right and what is wrong, what is virtuous and what is not, what is valuable and what is not. It is inspirational knowing, I contend, that is the source of what have long been termed deontological ethics – those ethics concerned with 'innate' rights and duties (in contrast to those consequentialist ethics that are concerned with rights and wrongs as they relate to the impacts that they have).

A Systemic Perspective

Imagine now that the four, somewhat instrumentally structured domains which have been described above as separate and diverse processes are but sub-processes (dynamic sub-systems) inextricably integrated within a coherent whole 'learning system'. Imagine further that such a system, involving either only ourselves as individuals or many individuals united in collective discourse, is itself inextricably connected with the rest of the world about us. We would then have, in Gregory Bateson's (1972) memorable phrase, a true and vibrant ecology of mind: a unity of the human mind with the rest of nature which owes its existence and creativity to its sheer diversity.

A systemic perspective on learning and its relationship with the sort of cultural unity across the globe that is sought through diversity begins to emerge. As Colin N. Power so rightly emphasises in his chapter in this volume, this is not the 'search for a single global blueprint', but the quest for 'ways by which diverse cultural groups can live together'. The relevance of a systemic perspective to this odyssey is that, as mentioned above, the very essence of systems theory is that the coherence and integrity of the whole come through what we might refer to as 'distinctions of difference' between the parts. If all the parts of a system were the same, it would not be a system – it would be a blob, or, if people, a mob!

Let me now take an introductory pass at the systemic essence of the learning/knowing process that has been elaborated so far by characterising a novel situation in which I might find myself as an individual, and through which I want to 'learn myself forward' into improved circumstances – in other words, to adapt myself or to change the situation in which I find myself, and/or to co-adapt in such a way that I focus on the interrelationship between myself and the world about me.

Starting, for the sake of convenience, with the experiential process (from now on referred to as the experiential sub-system of a 'whole' learning system), I firstly engage with some problematic situation or other in such a manner that I can make as many observations about it as possible, and from as many different perspectives as I can muster. At some point in this process, I will feel a need to shift from the concrete world of the situation I am experiencing to indulge in some abstract thoughts about what I am experiencing – I will feel an urge to resolve an internal systemic tension of difference between the process of sensing and that of making sense. It will take time for a picture to emerge in my mind, and I will possibly need to fluctuate between these processes of observing and thinking a number of times as I seek to reconcile the concrete with the abstract. It will usually be to my advantage to engage my propositional knowing sub-system during this engagement with the experiential process, as the thoughts, concepts or theories of others may well be of considerable assistance to me in my sense-making. And it may be that I need new practical knowledge as well at this point – to enable me to access a new source of knowledge such as a web-based data bank at a specialised Internet site, for instance. It is not difficult to conceive of this process involving three learning sub-systems (diverse ways of knowing) as a complex and very dynamic and interactive weaving between the 'weft' and the 'warp' of a three-dimensional tapestry.

There comes a moment when a further internal tension of difference makes itself felt with a need to shift from 'finding out' to 'taking action' to improve the original problematic situation. This is not an uncommon progression in a rational decision-making situation, with further tensions being generated between the need to plan action and action itself. The added involvement of practical learning at this stage in the experiential process is again indicated – once again illustrating the interdependencies among different learning sub-systems.

More often than not, however, the situations we find ourselves trying to improve extend 'beyond pure reason'. The first three interactions might well indicate what it is that *can* be done to improve a situation, while revealing little about what it is that *should* be done. It is thus vital that the learner disengage from the rational sub-systems at some point prior to planning the action, to allow the involvement of the inspirational sub-system and to give access to those innate insights that will add moral/ethical/aesthetic dimensions to the decision-making process. It is in this manner that we can envisage the learning system interrelating all four different sub-systems in an even more miraculous weaving – this time in four dimensions.

The indications are that at the early stage of appreciating these distinctions, a learner needs to be quite conscious of the 'mechanics' of change from one sub-system to another, just as he or she must be conscious of the need to integrate the sub-systems into a coherent 'whole' process. But as the learner matures, his or her learning system starts to assume vital self-organising dynamics, equivalent to the way one learns to integrate reading musical notations with manipulating fingers and, if relevant, patterns of breathing to create a seamless process (system) when making music.

It is this very consciousness about the nature of the learning processes and how they might be integrated together that adds the next level of complexity to a learning system. To know about the process of knowing, we need to engage with what a systems perspective would suggest is a 'higher order' of knowing. One of the wonderful talents of human beings is that they are able to know about knowing. In her discussion of this phenomenon, Karen Kitchener (1983) refers to this 'higher order of cognitive processing' as meta-cognition, and we can adopt that prefix here in referring to meta-knowing or meta-learning.

With this notion, we introduce a further dynamic into knowing systems as they learn how to monitor effectively their own processes. Just as I go about my knowing, so, too, I can go about evaluating how I am going about that knowing! Indeed, the ability to meta-know adds a vital new source of diversity to the learning system. With time, this systemic process, too, becomes self-organising and seamless, but at the initial stages of its introduction it must be handled as instrumentally as each of the other dimensions mentioned to this point.

Epistemic Development

It is timely now to add yet further complexity to the emerging knowing system by incorporating a third order of learning that Kitchener, from her concern with cognitive processing, labelled epistemic-cognition. Following her logic here, we can embrace the term epistemic-knowing (and learning) as that function that allows us to come to know about the nature of knowledge and the assumptions that we make about it as we go about our 'finding out' activities – whether, for instance, we believe that all knowledge is contextual and that truth is but a relative concept, or that all 'real' knowledge is truly objective. As Richard Bernstein (1983) presents it, there is clearly a very significant 'distinction of difference' between these two epistemological positions. The objectivist position reflects the conviction that 'there is or must be some permanent, ahistoric matrix or framework to which we can ultimately appeal in determining the nature of rationality, truth, reality, goodness or rightness'. The relativist position reflects the absolute opposite position – 'in the final analysis all such concepts (rationality, truth, goodness, etc.) must be understood as relative to a specific conceptual scheme, theoretical framework, paradigm, form of life, society or culture'. These distinctions are of profound importance with respect to arguments about 'unity in diversity' and the nature of critical learning systems, particularly as they relate to our abilities to assume a systemic perspective in the first place.

Marcia Salner (1986) has had some very important things to say about epistemological differences and their significance to epistemic-knowing, particularly with respect to the development of what she refers to as systemic capabilities. As she reports it, it is only when we assume the position of contextual relativism that we seem able to accept systems ideas, theories or principles, or to use systems methodologies with any conviction. Based on both her own empirical observations and a hypothesis developed by William Perry (1970), she suggests a need for involvement in a developmental process through which we shift our position from the prevailing one of 'dualism' (equivalent to objectivism) to that of 'contextual relativism'.

Our 'model' of a critical learning system not only has now acquired three dimensions of 'orders' or 'levels' of knowing (knowing in its four forms, meta-knowing and epistemic-knowing), but also has assumed a new dynamic as a developmental process through time. To this point we have conceived of the dynamics inherent in the model as a reflection of 'tensions of difference' (a) *within* any one level of knowing – for example, between finding out and taking action – and then (b) *between* the three levels of knowing. Now we must add a further dynamic between 'objective dualism' and 'contextual relativism', with this reflecting an actual process of development. It is as if the knowing/learning system that is the individual is capable of self-organisation through self-interrogation and development as it 'pulses between states' (as driven by tensions of difference) in the continuous process of adaptation to the environments about it. These adaptations must include making profound changes to itself with respect to changing both the way knowing is accomplished and epistemological perspectives.

If all that seems complicated, there is more to confound yet as we turn to paradigms and world-views, and to knowing as a social act.

Paradigms and World-Views

The concept of paradigm was first promoted by the philosopher of science Thomas Kuhn (1970), who defined it as that 'entire constellation of beliefs, values and techniques and so on shared by the members of a given community'. Epistemologies as sets of assumptions about the nature of knowledge are certainly included within such 'constellations of beliefs', but so, too, are other sets of philosophical assumptions – including ontologies (beliefs about the nature of nature) and axiologies (beliefs about human nature that are grounded in the particular sets of values that are held). All of these dimensions, minus 'techniques and so on', are components of world-views or *Weltanschauungen* – those intellectual/normative frameworks through which we filter our experiences of the world about us. Paradigms are world-views in action.

It is with world-views that we concern ourselves when talking of values in education, particularly with respect to their role in knowing – essentially as inspirationally derived influences on thought and thoughtful action. All of us, as individual learning systems, are characterised by the world-views which we embrace, the filters that we use to shape the way we both sense and make sense of the world about us. We are who we are as a result of their influence. It was the American philosopher, C. West Churchman (1971), who, drawing on ideas presented by other philosophers such as Heidegger, claimed that it is the ability to hold on to different, preferably conflicting, world-views at the same time that marks the mature individual. This is a wonderful example of the significance of 'tensions of difference' interacting in ways to generate a coherent and 'developed' whole. We are mature when we have learned not only how to appreciate different perspectives, but how to accommodate them, too.

This proposition has further significance when we explore the second part of Kuhn's definition above, which refers to 'sharing among members of communities'. Paradigms, as Kuhn envisaged them, are socially held. We must therefore now extend all the ideas that have been related so far to the individual, as a knowing/learning system, to groups of individuals – or knowing/learning collectives. And to do so, it makes sense to return to the central importance of the call for 'unity through diversity' and, in particular, to the application of Churchman's logic concerning maturity.

It can now be proposed that differences in perspectives (world-views) within communities are not only to be expected, but are essential if such collectives of 'knowing individuals' are to develop both the integrity of coherence and the dynamic of adaptability. Systemic unity, in this context of creative (= critical) tensions of difference, depends on diversity, but comes only with maturity.

Communities – be they the inhabitants of a single village or of an entire river catchment area, the pupils and teachers of a school, the members of a particular professional group or a cluster of folk within particular institutions or organisations, members of particular ethnic or racial groups, or the population of a nation as a whole – can be conceived of as entire knowing/learning systems: collections of people with significant differences between them, seeking to know how to adapt to the ever changing world about them collaboratively. And if this is a sensible proposition, it indicates a number of vitally important issues with respect to how education should proceed.

In this regard, it is appropriate at this point to move from the abstract to the concrete by exploring some of the lessons that have been learned from an evolving set of innovations in higher education that have characterised the 'teaching' of agriculture and rural development at Hawkesbury over the past two decades. It is important, first, to set the context for this discussion.

The Hawkesbury Context

At first sight, agriculture might seem to be a very unusual and unexpected vehicle for educational innovation. As a human endeavour, it has a pervasive image of conservatism, while its academic perspective, when considered at all, is that of an applied, and essentially natural, science. Agricultural science graduates, so the claim runs, typically have a low social profile as they go quietly about their business within a characteristically non-reactionary rural sector. A more careful analysis, however, will reveal a quite different picture for, in fact, agricultural educators have pioneered many radical innovations in education.

At its establishment in 1891, Hawkesbury Agricultural College was charged with the responsibility of bringing education in the sciences to the farmers of the colony of New South Wales. Given the rural culture that was pervasive at the time and the particular environmental and socio-economic conditions that prevailed, this was a remarkably radical innovation. The decade of the 1890s was a time of great drought in Australia and of the ravages of pests such as the rabbit and the prickly pear cactus. It was also a time of economic hardship – associated particularly with depressions in world commodity prices – and of post–gold rush property speculation. Finally, it was a period of acute industrial unrest, as manifested by shearers' strikes, and of social unrest that flowed from the confluence of all of the above.

Since the start of European settlement a hundred years or so earlier, Australian farmers had pioneered their own ways of doing things on this vast, arid continent. In the (mistaken) belief that the Aborigines had nothing to teach them, the settlers learned from their own experiences. Thus, the foundations for Australian agriculture were based not on adaptations and the development of indigenous practices, as in so many other places in the world, but on the direct importation of crop and livestock practices, and the plant and animals for them, from the Northern Hemisphere. The agricultural pioneers in this country developed superb skills of adaptation and technological innovation, with little if any awareness of science. Little wonder, then, that they were sceptical of the claims of the benefits of science promulgated by the staff at Hawkesbury and their research counterparts in the concurrently established Department of Agriculture (and Mines!).

Hawkesbury was established not as a Faculty within the autonomous University of Sydney, which was located a mere 40 miles or so within the city of Sydney, but as a College within the Colonial Department of Agriculture, on an estate of nearly four thousand acres. The idea was to combine lessons in theory with field experiences that reflected the application of those theories in practice. Most of the 'teachers' were also engaged in applied research and demonstration projects on the estate. The curriculum was thus an admixture of propositional and practical learning strategies. The propositional part was not confined to natural science subjects, but also included some 'social science' (financial management) and humanities (English language). Even sport was included as a formal subject. There was also a very pervasive thrust of experiential learning, as each 'class' of students had to assume responsibility for clearing and developing a portion of the estate, thereby transforming what was essentially a marsh into productive farming acreage and/or livestock paddocks.

The three-year diploma programme at Hawkesbury was revolutionary for its time, reflecting a number of elements that would still be regarded as radical today. Rare indeed, outside agriculture, are there contemporary curricula that have a balance between the natural and social sciences, or between propositional, practical and experiential learning strategies. From the late 1890s through to around the mid-1960s, Hawkesbury graduates had been presented with a curriculum that encouraged them to *learn to know* the theory of agriculture, to *learn to do* many of its theory-informed husbandries and to *learn to be* field development agriculturalists in action.

Hawkesbury was to remain, unashamedly, a teaching/ demonstrating institution within the Department of Agriculture of what later became the State of New South Wales for some 80 years following its establishment. Over later decades, however, it lost much of its momentum as a number of other institutions, including two new universities, also started to offer higher studies in agriculture within the State of NSW. Indeed, there is much to suggest that Hawkesbury 'lost itself' for a period of a decade from the early 1960s on. The new institutions posed a dilemma: should Hawkesbury try to mimic the universities and concentrate on essentially theoretical agricultural science (and propositional strategies to present it), or should it turn in the opposite direction and focus on practical agricultural technologies (leaving the theory to the universities)? Should it continue with diploma education or should it move towards degree-level programmes? Should it try to retain some research and work towards offering graduate programmes, or should it focus intently on teaching? Should it confine itself to agriculture and related subjects like food technology and home economics, or should it expand into a much broader academic profile? The constraints of being within the State *apparatchik*, however, rendered most of these debates mere rhetoric. To address them more freely, with an opportunity of doing something about it, the College would have to separate itself from the State agricultural bureaucracy. This it did when, during the early 1970s, Hawkesbury Agricultural College became an autonomous College of Advanced Education (CAE), with a vision to diversify markedly the disciplines it taught, and to become more 'university-like' in the future.

My appointment to the new CAE in 1978 was set within this context. Up to that point I had spent my career within universities, and at the time of my appointment as foundation Head of the new School of Agriculture within Hawkesbury, I was Dean of the Faculty of Rural Science at the University of New England. Rather than trying to foster a mimicry of New England's Faculty, however, I chose to encourage my new colleagues to return with me to the radical traditions of Hawkesbury's foundations, within a context set by a problematic future.

The late 1970s were once again a turbulent time in Australian agriculture. What was different about this situation, however, was that many of the new problems that were appearing had their origins in the techno-scientific solutions to yesterday's problems. Where science and its innovative technological applications had been the driving force behind the massively impressive growth in the productivity of agriculture since the turn of the century, that same force was now recognised as having a destructive side. The irony was that it took the very techniques of science to 'prove' that. Scientific research was revealing that certain 'developed' practices were resulting in the salinisation and acidification of the land in certain areas of the country. It was also revealing the fact that many pests and parasites were developing resistance to those very chemicals that had been introduced to kill them, while these same chemicals were also diffusing as pollutants into the atmosphere, ground water sources and even food items destined for human consumption.

In parallel with these ecological matters were socio-ecological concerns. The more productive the farmers became, the even more productive they had to become in order to keep pace economically, thus finding themselves caught in a vicious 'cost/price squeeze'. The more productive they needed to be, the more intensively they had to farm; the greater the level of intensification, the greater the damage being done to the environment and the higher the costs of repair. Also, the increased levels of intensification boosted the demand for capital and its substitution for labour, leading to greatly augmented financial stress in rural areas for both increasingly indebted farmers and unemployed 'capital-substituted' labour.

In the late 1970s, as we were planning our reforms at Hawkesbury with all this information as our context, we concluded that nothing less than a new paradigm was in order for Australian agriculture. Such a paradigm would need to appreciate that agriculture was no longer a straightforward study of applied natural sciences, but rather a field of immense complexity involving the social sciences and the humanities, as well. The focus was no longer simply one of production, but had to address, as well, all those ecological and socio-ecological outcomes of the previous approach. No longer could our students' studies be confined to learning about the technical feasibility and economic viability of what *could* be done; they would also need to learn how to judge the social and cultural desirability – and the ethical defensibility – of what *should* be done.

Curriculum Innovations

In the space available, it is impossible to catalogue all of the innovations that have occurred in agricultural education at Hawkesbury over the past two decades. For those interested in detailed accounts, a review of the major publications that flowed from the College can be found in Bawden (1999). Here I will concentrate on a number of matters that particularly express the concepts mentioned in the first part of this chapter. I will also confine my remarks to only one of a number of curricula that were developed for different course programmes.

It needs to be appreciated that the 40 or so academics who were involved in this development accepted it as a grand endeavour – a never ending critical action research project in which they would be participating with a wide network of 'actor stakeholders', including the students, collaborators from rural Australia and academics at other institutions. Over the years, this remarkable alliance would represent several hundred people at any one time, co-learning their way into 'improved futures'. And these co-learning, co-researching activities included some projects that were focused on improvements to the curriculum and to the organisation of the Faculty itself, as a response often to what was being learned from projects that concentrated on agricultural issues and broader situations in the rural environment. Discourse ruled the day, with all of us recognising not only that we did not have the answers with respect to desirable, feasible and defensible development, but also that we were genuinely unsure of the questions to ask in the first place.

Meanings, as experientially derived concepts qualified by inspirationally accessed insights, were accepted as the emergent properties of the coherent learning systems that we created. Consistent with the systemic thesis of 'unity through diversity', there would be no attempt to force a single world-view or intellectual perspective onto this dialogue. Instead, meaning would be allowed to emerge through the 'tensions of difference'. The greater the diversity, the greater the chance of emergent meaning. We were also prepared to be courageously innovative, and to act on the meanings that so emerged, even if such action appeared in contradiction to once cherished positions. It is interesting to now record, for instance, that the first intake of students was only in the fifth semester of the seven-semester course when the curriculum was changed in three very fundamental ways. To understand these changes, it is necessary, first, to describe the original format of the programme and the logic behind its development.

There were three pillars that formed the original foundations of the Hawkesbury curriculum. First, students would assume increasing responsibility for their own learning as they progressed through the seven semesters. Second, while the students would be exposed to propositional, practical and experiential learning strategies, it would be the last that would constitute the core pedagogical approach; the programme would be essentially an experiential one. Third, the perspective to be adopted for agriculture would be at the interface between nature and society, or, more specifically, at the point where natural ecosystems and social systems intersected. This third pillar was established in the belief that the explicit adoption of a systems perspective to agriculture would allow the students (and all of the other co-learners) to deal more adequately with the complexity of the matter at hand.

Academics would serve in three concurrent roles: as facilitators of group learning projects; as facilitators/advisors to a number of individual students and as content resource people. Every student would meet regularly with the facilitator to whom he or she had been allocated, both through individual appointment and in groups with their fellow allocatees. Particular faculty members were also accorded other duties that might include phase co-ordinator (the programme was divided into four phases), interest group co-ordinator, facility manager (which included farm and field resources), library liaison, staff professional development, rural network co-ordinator, newsletter editor, etc. The Faculty organised itself around a management matrix (with the Dean at a central node rather than at the top of a hierarchy) linking educational responsibilities with organisational-management roles.

The curriculum was organised around three pedagogical structures: (a) learning units that were presented by academic staff in a structured sequence of workshops that reflected the theme of the development and management of agricultural systems at the intersection between nature and society; (b) unsequenced but staff-structured learning experiences that were conducted periodically in response to either student demand or staff interest; and (c) unsequenced, student-structured learning experiences that were negotiated with the individual's facilitator and the year's co-ordinator as contracted learning projects.

During the first two semesters (phase one) of the programme, the approximate balance of the three strategies was 50 per cent staff-structured, sequenced units; 20 per cent staff-structured, periodic experiences; and 30 per cent student-structured, contracted learning projects. In the third semester (phase two), this balance shifted approximately to 30/30/40. The fourth semester (phase three) was spent almost entirely with one of the rural collaborators, with occasional interactions with faculty members, so the balance was essentially 0/10/90. The proportional representation of the different strategies in the final two semesters (phase four) of the programme was typically of the order of 0/20/80. During this last phase, supported by appropriate resource people back in the Faculty, students would conduct three or four self-directed, but contracted, projects (either as individuals or as members of a project team) with clients in the 'real world' beyond the campus.

A basic matrix of competencies was used as the framework around which the programme was organised, and this emphasised the focus of the course as the continuing development of the professional 'praxis' (theory- and value-informed practice) of each individual learner. Each student was expected to be aware not only of what he or she was learning about agricultural development, but also of how that learning was being achieved, and what impacts that was having on his or her own professional and personal development. Students were thus being asked to be involved in, and actively reflective about, learning, meta-learning and epistemic-learning.

The competency matrix included the three elements of effective communication, learning autonomy and systems agriculture (which included the essential 'content' of the learning), expressed across cognitive (knowledge-based), affective (value-based) and conative (action-based) domains. Subject disciplines were not taught as such at any time through the programme. Nor were conventional tests or formal examinations conducted. Rather, key concepts were presented in workshop format, written manuals (AgPaks) or text references, in the context of their relevance to some issue or theme. Assessment was based essentially on how students illustrated their understanding of concepts through their application in practice. Assessments, therefore, assumed the flavour of validations and were both formative at various points throughout the semester and summative at the end of each phase, when each student had to make both written and oral cases supporting an application to advance to the next phase. The competency matrix provided the organising principles for these presentations. A similar process occurred at the end of the programme, when students would apply to graduate, based on a case which not only reflected the work of the final phase, but also reviewed the student's praxial development across the entire four phases of the programme.

In 1983, only two years after the initial student intake, three major modifications were made to the programme. These are important to highlight here as they reflect a number of the essential matters raised earlier in this chapter. All were basically related to the 'discovery' – by two senior members of our Faculty, Bob Macadam and Roger Packham – of the work of Professor Peter Checkland and his colleagues at the University of Lancaster in England with what they referred to as 'soft systems methodology' (SSM). Rather than focusing on systems 'out there' in the real world, as we at Hawkesbury were doing in our degree programme, with emphasis on social, natural and agricultural systems, SSM focused on 'human activity systems', which were abstract constructs of the mind. These constructs, furthermore, were reflections of the particular world-views of those doing the construing; different world-views would reveal different activity systems. Most importantly, the methodology was, itself, a human activity system, reflecting, as Checkland (1981) declared, the shift in systemicity (the systems essence) from the real world to the process of inquiry into the world. SSM, which had been generated through an action research project conducted at Lancaster over several years, was seen by those who had developed it as a learning system.

Our two Hawkesbury colleagues chose to introduce SSM to the rest of the faculty in a most innovative and, ultimately, extremely significant manner. Involving a number of senior students in their research team, and using the formal soft systems methodology, they conducted an action research project into the Faculty itself (Macadam 1985). The conceptual models that they generated of our Faculty as a human activity system were then used as a vehicle for Faculty-wide debates about desirable and feasible changes to a wide range of its activities, including the design and conduct of the curriculum. A number of perceptive insights that emerged through these debates provided the conceptual foundations for the three curriculum modifications that were to be adopted and then retained over the next 10 years.

The first realisation was that students, in the final phases of their programme, would benefit enormously from involvement in formally planned participative action-research projects, which would be designed around a particular systems methodology (not necessarily SSM). The focus of these projects, which would be conducted in collaboration with a 'real world' client co-researcher, would be on systemic improvements to a 'messy' situation that the client considered to be problematic to him or her. These became known as 'situation improvement projects', and they persist in the curriculum to this day, albeit, over recent years, in a substantially modified form.

The second realisation followed from the first: if students were to conduct 'situation improving', participative action-researching projects in their senior year, using systems methodologies, such methodologies would need to be introduced as early as possible in the programme. This logic led to the significant insight that the experiential learning process, with its flux between finding out and taking action, and its alternation between concrete experience and abstract conceptualisation, could itself be perceived as a learning system. Furthermore, the soft systems methodology and, indeed, most research and development methodologies could be seen to be variations on the experiential learning theme. That logic could, therefore, be presented to the students from the

very start of their programme, with the experiential process
being portrayed as an essential precursor for a number of
methodologies that could be constructed from it. This realisation
also emphasised the significance of the involvement of the students in group learning/researching projects as early as possible
in their programme.

The third realisation followed on from the previous two.
Rather than structure the first year of the programme around a
sequence of 'fact-based' projects emanating from systems 'out
there', it now made more sense to re-design that phase as a pro-
gressive series of problem-based projects with the systems
emphasis on the process of learning. The students would thus be
involved in a sequence of projects of increasing complexity and
messiness as they moved through their first year. In this manner,
it was argued, they would come to understand the need for different methodologies for different circumstances, and, especially,
to appreciate the need for systemic approaches once the issues
got really complex and messy. The systemicity would be transferred from the 'world out there' to the 'system of inquiry into it'.
Students would learn about the emergent quality of meaning and
the importance of diversity to this process through learning to
practise discourse, that is, to invent and ask novel questions, and
not just answer conventional ones.

With all of these modifications in place, the final realisation
was that the whole Faculty and all of the activities in which it
engaged, on and off campus, could be seen and valued from a
critical learning system perspective. We were, indeed, learning
how to be systemic and how to help others do likewise – but the
question remained with respect to the impact of all this.

A Word about Outcomes

There can be no doubt whatsoever that, over the past decade or so,
Australian agriculture has come to reflect a systemic appreciation
of its own nature and issues of concern. It is impossible to state
with any confidence, however, the precise role which Hawkesbury graduates, Faculty and the network of collaborating farmers
have had on this shift of perspectives. Although some formal eval-
uations of the graduates have been conducted, the results, as one
would anticipate, are equivocal. Not surprisingly, the situation is
immensely complex, with the Hawkesbury initiatives being

paralleled by a *worldwide* call for more sustainable forms of food production, more ecologically benign agricultural practices and more responsible and ethically defensible forms of land management and resource development. From all accounts, Hawkesbury graduates have been in the thick of it. They are very well represented in employment associated with land care and catchment management, two fields of systemic expression in agriculture. They are also very evident in areas concerned with rural community development, and as teachers of agriculture and development. And in all of these arenas, they appear across the spectrum from operational, through managerial to policy-making levels. The academics, too, have been prominent in the emerging systemic face of agriculture, not only in this country, but internationally as well. Interestingly enough, their reputation is as much associated with curriculum reform and transformation in higher education as it is with agriculture and related fields.

Over recent years, the radical edge of the Hawkesbury experience in education for agriculture and rural development has all but dulled. The current undergraduate programmes are little different from those found anywhere else, with the focus on experiential processes and systems methodologies now difficult to discern. Ironically, given its original mission to be 'university-like', most of the demise of the innovation has occurred since the College was integrated, along with two other CAEs, into the University of Western Sydney in 1988. As that large institution has grown and developed, so the pressures to conform have been applied. From its position as a highly unorthodox and innovative 'node' at the 'boundary of the institution', the Faculty of Environmental Management and Agriculture, as it has become, has been drawn increasingly into the conventional mainstream. This has been no one's fault. It is just the way that the system has felt obliged to respond to pressures from its environment. These pressures have included changing conditions within the institution itself, the needs and wishes of a new generation of students (now substantially responsible for the costs of their own education), and the attitudes and policies of governments of the day.

Yet, even as the focus on undergraduate curriculum innovation has dimmed at Hawkesbury, so the post-graduate programmes, which also now accommodate research degrees, continue to flourish. Such is the nature of complex adaptive systems: something always emerges when there is requisite diversity – even peace!

References

Bateson, G. 1972. *Steps Toward an Ecology of Mind*. Ballentine: New York.

Bawden, R.J. 1999. *A Cautionary Tale: The Hawkesbury Experience*. Wageningen University Press: Wageningen, The Netherlands.

Bernstein, R.J. 1983. *Beyond Objectivism and Relativism*. University of Pennsylvania Press: Philadelphia.

Checkland, P.B. 1981. *Systems Thinking: Systems Practice*. John Wiley: New York.

Churchman, C.W. 1971. *The Way of Inquiring Systems*. Basic Books: New York.

Hutchins, R. 1976. *The Higher Learning in America*. University of Chicago Press: Chicago.

Kitchener, K. 1983. Cognition, meta-cognition and epistemic-cognition: a three-level model of cognitive processing. *Human Development*, vol. 26.

Kolb, D. 1984. *Experiential Learning: Experience as the Source of Learning and Development*. Prentice-Hall: Englewood Cliffs, NJ.

Kuhn, T. 1970. *The Structure of Scientific Revolutions*. Routledge and Kegan Paul: New York.

Macadam, R. 1985. Introducing problem-based learning into a curriculum – the Hawkesbury experience. In D. Boud (ed.). *Problem-Based Learning in Education for the Professions*. HERDSA: Sydney.

Perry, W. 1970. *Forms of Intellectual and Ethical Development in the College Year*. Holt, Rinehart and Winston: New York.

Reason, P., and Heron, J. 1986. Research with people: the paradigm of co-operative experiential inquiry. *Person-Centred Review*, vol. 1.

Salner, M. 1986. Adult cognitive and epistemological development. *Systems Research*, vol. 3, no. 4.

Wilber, K. 1997. *The Eye of Spirit: An Integral Vision for a World Gone Mad*. Shambhala: Boston.

— Seven —

EDUCATING FOR A HUMANE SOCIETY

Elizabeth M. Campbell

Introduction

The term 'humane' which appears in the title of this chapter is intended to encompass four values that were listed separately in the early stages of the Campbell, McMeniman and Baikaloff study (1992), but clustered together in the multidimensional scaling exercise (Chapter 3): *equitable treatment of all, care and compassion, empathy* and *co-operation*. The aim of this chapter is to consider how education can contribute to the development of a society in which these values feature prominently within individual and group relationships. According to Norman Graves (1988: 44), such a society 'is one in which the basic human emotions of love for one's fellows, and compassion for the less fortunate, are very much alive. It is also a [society] in which institutions have developed which make possible or facilitate mutually support-ive relationships'.

The need for the strengthening of such values is obvious, for our 'global village' is replete with threats that have the capacity to destroy us all. On the international stage, we have, for exam-ple: countries in which poverty is so extreme that the populations have no choice but to sacrifice the future of themselves and their children in order to survive in the present; countries in which life-threatening diseases are rampant, and only the toughest of the young grow into healthy adults; countries in which 'ethnic cleansing', genocide and other brutal crimes against humanity are prevalent practices. Similarly, on the Australian national stage, we have, for example: thousands of homeless youth; high and rising incidences of violent crimes and drug abuse; an alleged world-record high rate of suicide, especially among 15- to 24-year-old males; and deep-rooted divisions between indigenous and non-indigenous peoples which must be bridged before Australia can play a full part in the community of nations.

It should be acknowledged at the outset that, as the 1989 UNESCO Report (*Learning to Care: Education for the Twenty-First Century*) stated, the foundations for the development of humane individuals will be laid not in educational institutions, but in families and other early care-giving settings: 'The development of self-esteem is important before children can venture into the world with confidence and develop a caring attitude to others.... In the family situation the basic building blocks for a caring character are formed. These include trust, hope, love, respect, and optimism.' And families, or their surrogates, are likely to continue to be of paramount importance in this regard. The implication of this is that professional educators, particularly those specialising in early childhood, can make their greatest contribution to early character building by working in a close, supportive relationship with parents and surrogate parents.

In many indigenous societies, including Australian-Aboriginal, as Margaret Valadian (1999) has reminded us, parents could expect support, too, from the immediate neighbourhood, which constituted a genuine 'community', characterised by caring and mutually supportive relationships. The non-indigenous Australian society has seldom achieved this measure of community, although, as Walter (1990: 10) reports, this was its vision during a brief period following the Second World War, when the family was seen not as an isolated unit, but as an integral part of a much greater whole – as part of a neighbourhood, of a town, of a region, each of which possessed some sense of unity and common life. That vision has long since been replaced, and, except in a few instances, local neighbourhoods in non-indigenous societies are scarcely even pale reflections of it. Not surprisingly, what exists now exerts only a vestigial moral influence, as evidenced in the following statement by Richard Eckersley (1990), in which he draws upon the findings of a 1989 study by Mackay Research:

> ... the most interesting finding of the study ... concerns young people's moral sense. Mackay found that they believe that moral values

are in decline, and often find it hard to identify an accepted moral framework within the community – unless they are religious. Moral responsibility to 'the group' is much stronger than to 'the community': 'Thus the ethical sense is rooted in a social sense, but that social sense is very limited, very transient, and very fragile. Lacking a broader sense of "the community", many young people have difficulty in establishing an ethical framework which has any application beyond the boundaries of their own immediate circle of friends.'

Not only is the wider society an untrustworthy developer of humane values in the young, it is likely to exert a negative influence by way of a philosophy which espouses the view that individuals aggressively pursuing their own economic interests will automatically create the best society. As Colin N. Power states in Chapter 2, '[T]he values and assumptions of [this] model are badly flawed. The type of development they promote is neither equitable nor sustainable.' Similarly, Paige Porter (1997: 94) argues: 'The cement of a society must be, at minimum, a concern for the rest of the group. Upon this base must we build the empathy – and compassion – without which we cannot claim to be a socially just society. Individual achievements and competition are important, but they will not, on their own, sustain, much less energise, a common concern and purpose.' Finally, Norman Graves (1988: 48) regrets that, in many societies, the notion of a caring community is covertly, if not overtly, discouraged in the interests of greater economic efficiency.

The upshot of all this is that education (together, in some cases, with voluntary youth associations) is likely to be the main agency supporting the efforts of the home to nurture the caring propensities of the young. In addition to working collaboratively with parents and parent surrogates, educational professionals can contribute to the nurturance of humane individuals by ensuring that their own settings are free of negative, inhumane elements; are endowed with a generous supply of positive, humane elements; and include, within their curricula, experiences that are more deliberately designed to nurture aspects of personality, knowledge and skill associated with commitment to equitable, caring, compassionate, empathic and co-operative actions. The beauty of these 'school-based' measures is that they are not merely supportive of home efforts, but are also essential for the achievement of what many see as education's *primary* concern – the effective development of a wide range of intellectual capacities and skills – for inhumane elements are inhibitors, and humane ones facilitators, of this concern. Thus the situation is a 'reciprocal' win/win/win one: the parents win by having *their* efforts supported; the professionals win by having *their* overall aims supported; and the young win by having 'significant others' working in partnership to foster *their* development.

The intention in the next four sections is to discuss the listed educational contributions in turn. Although it is possible to distinguish among these measures for purposes of discussion, in practice they are likely to be interrelated, and it will be difficult for me to retain clear and clean distinctions among them.

Working in Partnership with Parents and Parent Surrogates

According to Margaret Henry (1996, 1999), professional educators have not been universally successful in supporting parents and parent surrogates as they strive to develop the foundations of humane values in their children. She attributes this to a tendency on the part of the professionals to enact the role of 'colonisers', laden with a bounty of expertise, rather than that of 'partners', engaged in a joint venture of meeting 'reciprocal' needs. Her answer to what she calls the 'coloniser's conundrum' has been to design and offer an innovative, teacher education course – *Working with Parents and Community* – which combines the first three of Erikson's (1950) challenges facing the young child (the building of trust, autonomy and initiative) with a number of facilitative parental behaviours arising out of reviews by Hess (1971), Amato (1987) and Ochiltree and Edgar (1995) – warmth, expression of high regard, attentiveness/engagement, consistency, explanatory regulatory strategies, encouragement of independence, encouragement of achievement, talking *with* rather than *to* and provision of stimulating resources. She concludes by encapsulating the thinking of Erikson and Hess within three major dimensions – *responsiveness, control* and *involvement* – which, she proceeds to show, are as equally applicable to adult-adult relationships as they are to adult-child ones.

The *Working with Parents and Community* course requires education students, over a 12-week period, to carry out with a parent/parents: (1) an individual episode and (2) a group activity aimed at providing them with intensive practice in, and analysis of, 'reciprocal relationships' in which not only the students give something to parents and children, but also parents and children give something to students. The project begins with the student exploring the needs of participants (self, parents and child), and formulating appropriate aims for each on the basis of these needs. Then follow the creation and implementation of a programme designed to achieve the aims, and, finally, an assessment of outcomes. (Full details are available in Henry 1999.) As Henry explains, '*Working with Parents and Community* courses offer students the analytic tools to tease out the components of reciprocity and to see how working reciprocally with parents adds not just to children's resources, not just to parents' resources, but also to their own resources as teachers. For students, that is the transformational outcome.'

It will be clear from the above that *Working with Parents and Community* aims not only to strengthen the confidence which the parents and education students have in themselves as parents and teachers, respectively, but to provide them, and the children, with the educational experience of gaining insight into the nature of reciprocity and the benefits to be gained from establishing situations in which *everyone* wins. These are valuable lessons which can be transferred to many different situations within the realm of developing humane values.

Removal of Inhumane Elements

When educational institutions as we know them today were first established, they were modelled on the factories in which the 'masses' toiled. Unfortunately, in a vastly different age, they still retain some inappropriate factory elements. Among these are *densely populated schools* and *classes*. In a number of naturally occurring 'field experiments', Campbell (1981, 1990) has shown that, in comparison with students in small schools and small classes, those in large ones participate in fewer activities, occupy fewer key positions, experience less support from teachers and peers, are less supportive of fellow students, have less responsibility for activities and display more withdrawn and aggressive behaviour and less time on task. These behaviours are not mysterious psychological outcomes, but rather simply *processes* which must occur within learning settings that vary in size. They do, however, initiate a chain of events that can be shown to extend, through primary and secondary consequences, to important educational outcomes, such as concern for others, reactions to individual differences and support of fellow students.

The issues of large schools and classes are important, but a phenomenon that might be considered to have an even greater effect upon the development of individuals is the nature of the relationship among learners in the course of learning. Three such relationships are commonly identified: *individualistic* – when the achievement of one member is largely unrelated to the success or failure of others; *co-operative* – when the attainment of goals requires the co-operation of members, without which no one can achieve; *competitive* – when, to some degree, the success of one member is dependent upon the failure of others. It is common knowledge that teaching styles around the world tend to be biased in favour of competition and individualism (Berrell, 1993; Berrell and Gloet 1995). It is, however, small-group co-operative learning that has been found to be most effective with respect to developing commitments to principles such as equity, respect for others, moral obligation and the like (Northey 1990; Sharan 1980; Slavin 1983). Although Northey and others in this research field do not use these categories, it is convenient to consider their findings under the headings that feature in the school-size studies, namely, process behaviours, primary consequences, secondary consequences and distal outcomes. Thus:

Process behaviours: In comparison with students engaged in small-group co-operative learning, those taught by whole-class competitive, or individual, methods will almost inevitably be less active, participate at a lower level ('customer' or 'onlooker', rather than 'leader' or 'functionary'), display less co-operative behaviour, interact with other students less frequently, be involved in less decision-making. (Again, these are not outcomes in the usual sense of this term, but simply behaviours that are essential to the functioning of different learning settings.)

Primary consequences: In comparison with students engaged in small-group co-operative learning, those taught by whole-class competitive, or individual, methods are likely to have a weaker sense of being needed, display less empathic behaviour, display less respect for others, be more critical of others, have a weaker sense of empowerment, have a weaker sense of ownership of process and end products, have a weaker sense of responsibility.

Secondary consequences: In comparison with students engaged in small-group co-operative learning, those taught by whole-class competitive, or individual, methods are likely to develop weaker and less varied social skills, be less conscious of the interdependence of people, have weaker and less varied self-concepts, have weaker senses of personal control, be less conscious of the benefits of diversity and plurality.

Distal outcomes: In comparison with students engaged in small-group co-operative learning, those taught by whole-class competitive, or individual, methods are likely to display less commitment to equality, equity, participation, co-operation, peace, the environment, basic social and economic rights, responsible economic development, obligation to – and respect for – others. This is an impressive list of important, long-term developments, and it would strengthen my case greatly if the research findings supported them unequivocally, but I am not completely sure that they do. Be that as it may, the secondary consequences listed, although not as impressive, are very worthy achievements, and they seem to be well supported by the research findings.

Clearly, it is important that a competitive psychological climate should not be allowed to pervade school and classroom processes, despite pressures from the 'real world'. In one of his many recent books, the late W.N. Oats writes of his appointment as Headmaster to Kings College, and of his successful efforts to dismantle the elements of competition that had survived even within that small, family-type school (1986: 124):

> I believed that the competitive spirit, whatever the support given it by the business world, needed no encouragement. In this respect, advice given recently to educators by a business tycoon was appallingly direct and brutally frank. 'Go for the jugular', he urged. This was the spirit to be inculcated in schools, he said, if we were not to slide into a third-world status. It seemed not to have occurred to him that our malaise as a country was not lack of competitiveness, but unwillingness to co-operate, with management and unions equally guilty.

A third feature of educational institutions that exerts a counter-productive effect upon all aspects of human development, and more obviously so than the first two, is bullying, which is alleged to be rife in schools from kindergarten to secondary (Slee and Rigby 1991). In a review of the effects of bullying upon the bullied,

Toni Michael (1999: 5) writes: 'If bullying is long-standing and persistent, the long-term consequences for the victims are distressing.... [T]hey often feel isolated by their experience and wonder why they have been stigmatised. They may become withdrawn and less willing to take social and intellectual risks. Their feelings of self-reproach are part of the reason why these children do not confide in their parents or teachers.' It would be surprising if these 'victims' *were* able to retain the mental energy needed to profit maximally from the offerings of the schools.

The above quotation from Michael has been taken from a report in which she outlines how one primary school, with which she was associated in the capacity of a parent, went about trying to minimise bullying. The account is valuable, not least because of the detail which Michael provides on the steps that she and her associates took in rallying support from the total 'school community'.

Anti-Bullying Programme: Action Plan

Definition (for use with the younger primary-school students): Bullying happens when one person or a group of people tries to upset another person by saying nasty or hurtful things to them again and again. Sometimes, bullies hit or kick people or force them to hand over money; sometimes they tease them again and again. The person who is being bullied finds it difficult to stop this happening and is worried that it will happen again. (It may not be bullying when two people of roughly the same strength have a fight or disagreement.)

Aims: To create a non-threatening environment for children, and involve the school community in processes to achieve this.

Steps taken:

1. Approach to Principal.
2. Raise awareness among: *teachers* and *non-teaching staff* (meeting plus group interviews), *parents* (letter to parents, parent meetings, and group interviews), *children* (poster competition, involve in mapping danger areas, involve in writing a story or drawing pictures, older children speaking with younger ones about their experiences, a questionnaire, group interviews), *local community* (parish newsletter, contact with police, contact with other schools and pre-schools, an information evening).
3. Establishment of Working Party with representation from all stakeholders.
4. Data-gathering: teacher observations in the playground, recording of all incidents, survey questionnaire to older children, group discussions with younger children.

5. Analysis of data and development of temporary strategies (recording all incidents, increased adult supervision in certain areas, reduction of amount of time spent in lines waiting for teachers and others).
6. Focus-group discussions with parents and staff to develop policy.
7. Keeping all parents informed on activities, and maintaining an open-door policy with respect to participation. (This allowed all members of the school community to feel a sense of ownership of the programme.)
8. Production of a booklet containing the policy statement, and an official launching of the booklet.
9. Evaluation: The incidents of bullying did diminish, but we discovered that raising awareness needs to be a continual process for the effectiveness of the programme to be long lasting.

Concluding statement: We may not be able to eliminate bullying, but we can successfully reduce the incidence and likelihood of it occurring in our schools. In the literature dealing with various methods of managing the problems of bullying, the following practices were found to be important: raising awareness to encourage participation, using a whole school-community approach, encouraging collaborative decision-making, empowering participants. Each of these featured in my work with the local primary school.

Before we can adequately change children's attitudes towards bullying, we must ask ourselves whether we identify more with the bully or the bullied. We can so easily dismiss children with phrases such as 'Don't tell tales', or 'Boys will be boys', which can convey the message that, at best, we do not take bullying seriously, and, at worst, that we positively endorse it. Do we regard victims as wimps, cry-babies or overprotected? Do we have a sneaking regard for children who 'can look after themselves' – who don't 'come whining all the time'. Until we challenge these kind of attitudes in ourselves, we will continue to give an inappropriate message to children about bullying.

Establishment of Humane Elements

It is *essential* to remove from learning settings those elements that are educationally counter-productive, but it is *not sufficient*. It is equally essential to ensure that positive elements feature, among which are respect for people, care, compassion, equitable treatment and the like. As long ago as 1966, James Coleman, in his seminal, nationwide study of American education, reported that student deficiencies in a range of intellectual and skill achievements could often be traced back to programmes which appropriately stressed traditional school competencies, but in which warm interpersonal relationships, concern for others, and general caring were absent. Not surprisingly, this finding has been confirmed in a large number of subsequent studies. Thus, Ramsay *et al.* (1983), in their comparison of 'successful' and 'unsuccessful' New Zealand schools (as assessed by a series of standardised tests of reading skills, listening skills and computation; results in the national School Certificate examination; rates of vandalism; levels of truancy and levels of control problems), reported that the existence of a supportive, caring environment in the 'successful' schools was *the* major distinguishing factor. The researchers concluded (294):

> The coherence of purpose we noted in 'successful' schools also had a common thread – the teachers in developing a community of interest demonstrated very clearly that they cared about children. This permeated the whole school, which had a pleasant, caring environment where ... pupils, parents and teachers worked together towards a common goal.... In general, a coherence of purpose had emerged, and the children appeared to be working happily in a friendly, non-threatening environment.

Malcolm Skilbeck endorses the Ramsay *et al.* finding when he states (1988: ii):

> The separation of caring from the fundamental purposes and values of education is disastrous ... the understanding and support for the individual implied by a commitment to caring is essential for success in the educational enterprise. This is true whether that education is at the early childhood stage, in maturity or the later years of life. It is true, likewise, whether we have in mind education focused on skills and values, knowledge or understanding, and regardless of the subject matter.

Following is an excellent example of an innovative educational programme, characterised by small, 'bonded' groups of students learning co-operatively within caring settings.

The Alternative Transition Programme

In 1980, the Australian Government made funds available to the States to enable them to provide 'alternative-transition' education to 'at risk' students who had completed Year 10 of schooling. The focus of this programme was intended to be threefold: provide work-oriented experiences, foster closer school-community relationships and enhance proficiency in basic literacy and numeracy. Almost without exception, however, the school co-ordinators of this programme decided that the pressing need of their students was for experiences that would promote personal development, life-role skills and specific vocational skills, in that order, and, given a high measure of autonomy, they proceeded to change direction a little by developing curricula to meet student needs as they saw them. As Norman Graves (1988: 48) remarks: 'If [teachers] hold on to the values that animate the caring community, then no edict or regulation can change that.... Alasdair MacIntyre put it less optimistically in his Richard Peters Lecture: "Teachers are the forlorn hope of Western Modernity."'

Early in 1981, Campbell was commissioned by the Australian Government to evaluate the accomplishments of this programme, and over the next few years he directed two investigations into it (Campbell and McMeniman 1983; Arunpairojana 1987). Because of the need for an early report, the former was a one-shot research study, involving *implicit* control groups, but the latter was a longitudinal one, involving carefully chosen, normal-type controls and conducted over a 12-month period. Findings from both studies are drawn upon in the following account.

Because of the actions taken by the co-ordinators 'at the coal-face', the alternative-transition programme provided an excellent opportunity to assess the effects, upon low-achieving students, of transferring from a course characterised by high academic demands, subject-oriented curricula, large classes (around 30 students), rigid timetables and multiple teachers to one characterised by low academic demands, modules-of-experience curricula, small classes (around 15 students), flexible and negotiable timetables, and often a single co-ordinator. Campbell and McMeniman (1983: 11) comment:

> The clearest message to emerge from this comparative survey of aims and curricula, is that the structures which have been set up to support and promote learning and development differ markedly. Within the mainstream courses, the learning environment appears somewhat rigid and unresponsive: the curriculum content and the method of acquiring it are pre-ordained, the educational pathways are few and narrow, boundaries of space and time are sharply defined, and the role of the learner is a subordinate one. By way of contrast, the alternative courses exhibit a flexible and responsive learning environment: there are several broad highways and a few seductive byways in

which students might linger, the structures seem to be capable of expansion and contraction according to the needs of the students, and the experiences progressively approximate the realities of the world beyond the school. It is clear that the alternative transition innovation has gone far beyond a mere change in the content of the curriculum to an assault upon the traditional structures represented by social organisation, timetabling, and use of spaces, as well as subject matter.

The 'alternative' students themselves, in questionnaires and interviews, tended to highlight the changed relationship between themselves and the teacher.

We have a close, relaxed relationship with the teacher. We are like one group. The teacher that we have is kind of a mate. He's a guy that you don't kind of look up to, you look straight across at; he's sort of more on your level, and you sort of get on reasonably well with him. It's like being a real human being, because in my other courses it was really never like person-to-person talking. It was always they were up there, and you were down here. With this group they talk to you as more of a friend than anything.

When you're in Years 8, 9, and 10, and even in the other senior years, the teachers don't regard you as people even. In this course we get on so good with teachers because they regard us like normal people, adults.

Most useful part of the course was the atmosphere – you were all together all the time and you got to know each other really well ... in the normal school they're trying to teach you things, to drum it into your head, they're not really concerned with what's going on in *your* head. But Mr. X [the co-ordinator] would sit down with you – he would talk to you more as a friend than as a teacher. Over the year, we developed into a pretty good group that was able to do things – for example, ringing up employers and seeking a job interview – on our own. We called ourselves the 'self-starters'! Mr X was always there in the background arranging things, but we were pretty much doing the front things ourselves.

To an unusually high degree, the alternative programme appeared to meet UNESCO's (1989: 11) recommendation that

Rather than considering how to prepare young people for the future, we need to think about preparing for the future with the help of young people through their active participation in and involvement with constructive and co-operative educational environments. In the classroom, a 'pedagogy of democratic fellowship' can be created in which children collaborate and support each other in their learning. Such classrooms can be mini social realities in which students assume different roles, including those of leadership. Teachers are facilitators, organizers and managers of the learning – in this way, they focus not so much on what they are to teach but on supporting their students' learning. In this way, values are imparted through action and interpersonal behaviour in the classroom.

The proof of the pudding, of course, is in the eating. What effect did the transition from mainstream to the alternative programme have upon personal-development outcomes which the co-ordinators valued so highly? Perhaps the most convincing evidence comes from the Campbell-supervised Arunpairojana Ph.D. study, which involved a comparison of four groups of students: *Group 1*: high achievers in Year 10 who proceeded to mainstream Year 11; *Group 2*: medium achievers in Year 10 who also proceeded to mainstream Year 11; *Group 3*: low achievers in Year 10 who were offered a place in the alternative programme, but elected to proceed, with their more highly achieving friends, to mainstream Year 11; and *Group 4*: low achievers in Year 10 who entered the alternative programme in Year 11. All four groups reported on the contribution of the courses to various aspects of their personal development on four occasions: near the end of Year 10, after three months in Year 11, after six months in Year 11 and after nine months in Year 11. On each occasion, raw scores from various aspects were converted to z-scores and summed with a constant weighting of unity. It is the composite means of these z-scores which feature in the table below:

Groups	Occasions			
	1	2	3	4
1 and 2 (mainstream)	0.54	0.24	0.43	0.37
3 (mainstream)	-0.08	-2.11	-2.00	-2.56
4 (alternative)	-1.06	2.00	2.42	2.31

It will be clear from the figures above that whereas the high and medium achievers (Groups 1 and 2) in Year 10 continued to report somewhat positively on their school influences in Year 11, the low achievers who elected to continue in the mainstream (Group 3) demonstrated dramatic disenchantment with the school's contribution to their personal development. By way of contrast, the low achievers in Year 10 who elected to enter the alternative programme (Group 4) underwent a meta-morphosis to surpass their highly achieving classmates in attributing positive contributions of the course to their personal development.

Of special significance for this chapter, both Arunpairojana (1987) and Campbell and McMeniman (1983) concluded that the more humane alternative programme was particularly effective in promoting values such as: *respecting the rights and freedoms of others; accepting the will of the majority; respecting groups with little power; respecting human life and dignity; caring for the sick, the poor and the aged;* and *valuing justice for everyone.* At the level of implementation, the alternative-transition programme might not have been as vocationally oriented as its political architects had hoped, but it was successfully addressing issues which are of even greater significance to us all.

Introduction of Curricula Deliberately Aimed at Developing Humane Values

To continue with the culinary metaphor, the icing on the cake occurs when – in addition to partnership with parents, the absence of inhumane elements and the presence of humane ones – curricula include experiences deliberately aimed at fostering cognitive, conative, skill and affective attributes associated with the development of humane relationships. Without suggesting that students are not learning from co-operative, humane experiences – the tenor of the above is that they *are* learning a great deal – the inclusion of curricular experiences concerned with thinking and knowing in the realm of humane values underscores the point that *learning* is a key concern of education. John Passmore (1985: 11) states this strongly:

> ... the crucial question is what [our young] have learnt.... What matters is how our young will act, what they will value, in that twenty-first century in which they will come to maturity and assume positions of authority....
>
> Unless their schooling makes some discernible difference to the ways in which in their adult life they confront problems, to what they value and what they resist, to the skills they display and the information they have at their disposal, to their openness to further learning, to their ability to engage in rational discussion, to the manner in which they respond to proposed innovations, we might as

well dismantle the whole expensive educational apparatus and look for some cheaper form of child-minding.

It is useful to take as a starting point here Richard J. Bawden's presentation, in Chapter 6, of a multidimensional model of knowing, involving four *forms* (propositional, practical, experiential and inspirational), three *orders* (the forms, meta-knowing and epistemic-knowing), *a process of development* (from 'objective dualism' to 'contextual relativism') and *world-views*. What are the implications of this model for a humane-values curriculum?

A few years ago, Brian V. Hill (1992: 7) went some way towards operationalising the Bawden conception when, referring to values education in general, he stated:

Values education should seek:

1. To enable students:
   (a) To acquire a representative knowledge base concerning the value traditions which have helped to form contemporary culture;
   (b) To enter with empathy into the perceptions and feelings of people who have been strongly committed to these traditions;
   (c) To develop skills of critical and appreciative values appraisal;
   (d) To develop and put into practice the skills of decision-making and value negotiation; and
2. To encourage students to develop a concern for the community and the care of its members.

The *knowledge base* calls for solid content related to the value systems abroad in pluralistic society. It is not to be merely head knowledge, but *understanding* coloured by feeling, the result of exercising *empathy* – trying to understand other people's motivations and views of the world from the inside. The *skills* to be practised include values appraisal, i.e. ethical skills as well as social skills. Furthermore, the development of these capacities is not just for show; it is meant to bear fruit in *action*.

Nicholas Burbules (1997: 111) goes even closer to Bawden's conception of knowing when discussing the issue of an educational programme for 'multiculturalism'. (Insertions in brackets connect to Bawden's concepts.)

It is not just a matter of … teaching *about* diverse cultures, traditions, or systems of belief. It is not just a matter of supplementing a standard curriculum with representative samplings from other points of view. It is not just a matter of introducing or displaying elements from other cultures, often out of context, for their exotic, colourful flavour. This sort of diversification of the curriculum [*forms of knowledge*] ... is really only a step, a means to something deeper and more important educationally. Tolerance of difference, or for that matter celebrations of difference, are not the ultimate educational outcomes we should be after; it is the critical re-examination of difference, the questioning of our own systems of difference, and what they mean for ourselves and for other people.... Education should not simply be about transmitting an existing system of belief and value, unchanged, from one generation to the next; there must be some room for questioning, re-interpreting, and modifying that system in light of a broadened understanding of where it fits in the context of a diverse, rapidly changing world.

One of the primary features of this world is the growing awareness of difference itself [*meta-knowing*] and a beginning to appreciate that questions about where those differences come from and how they come to mean what they do to different groups [*epistemic-knowing*] raise fundamental questions in turn about the world, and why we have come to settle on one account of it as opposed to another, depending on who we are and where we live [*process of development*].... This does not necessarily lead to relativism, in my view; but it does lead to appreciating the arbitrariness of at least part of what we take for granted about ourselves and about others, along with the realisation that from another frame of reference those assumptions will appear quite different [*paradigms and world-views*]. 'Multiculturalism', in this sense, is as much about a critical reflection upon our own culture, our art, our science, our ethics, and so on, as it is about the exploration of others'.

In the passage above, Burbules shows how the issue of multiculturalism can be explored at a *high educational* level by going beyond the mere transmission of conventional forms of knowledge concerning cultural differences to a sophisticated study of the nature and origins of difference, itself. With reference to this same issue of multiculturalism, Ramsay *et al.* (1983: 282–3) report that in their 'successful' schools, the teachers 'were not merely teaching *about* other cultures in a "museum box" sense, nor had they merely adjusted the environment to make culturally different children comfortable; rather they were attempting to produce learners who had competencies and ability to operate in two (or more) different cultures'. And they were achieving this by means of a 'lively treatment' of *cultural change, cultural interaction* and the *reciprocal nature of acculturation*.

It will be clear from these examples that the introduction of the Bawden-type 'systemic' thinking to issues such as multicultural-ism within the realm of humane values will lead to a much richer educational experience than is often provided. And there are lighthouse programmes which have set out to do this.

Looking at Ourselves and Others

At the 40th International Conference of WEF, David Woolman (1999) reviewed a number of US programmes on Schooling for Civility: Conflict Resolution Programs as a Response to Youth Violence. Among these was *Looking at Ourselves and Others* (US Peace Corps 1993), and because it seems to illustrate the educa-tional approach of Bawden, Burbules, and Ramsay *et al.* rather well, it is reproduced here, from the Woolman conference paper, in its entirety.

> Since 1961 the U.S. Peace Corps has placed volunteers in developing countries to work in agriculture, business, community development, education and health. The World Wise Schools program sponsored by the Peace Corps enables U.S. schools to connect with an inservice vol-unteer overseas in a reciprocal helping/learning relationship. Typically the class provides some support for a project conducted by the volun-teer whereas the class in turn learns much about the people and cul-ture of the country. To improve this learning partnership, Peace Corps has developed *Looking at Ourselves and Others*, a secondary level mini-curriculum unit which helps students recognize differences in perception, identify stereotypes, practice strategies for reducing stereotyping, define the meaning of culture and look at the role cul-ture plays in shaping the way we develop perceptions of ourselves and others. The program is geared for teaching about the ways that errors in reasoning and judgment form the basis for prejudicial thought that can lead to conflict.
>
> *Looking at Ourselves and Others* has three units. The first deals with facts, opinions and perceptions. It covers topics such as differences in perception, the relationship between actual knowledge and percep-tion, the role of predisposition in shaping perception, the process of rumor formation and distortion of facts, the distinction between fact and opinion and ways of testing the accuracy of generalizations. The second section is concerned with recognition and reduction of stereo-types. It explores the nature of prejudice, labeling, faulty generaliza-tion and media images of different groups. Other skills developed in this section are looking beyond the surface in forming opinions of others, recognizing that every person is valuable because they are

special and unique, and becoming proficient in using verbal rebuttal
of prejudicial statements by others. The last section works on building awareness of many aspects of culture so that students can better
understand how their own culture conditions perspectives and viewpoints about other cultures.

A reader who is familiar with Bawden's conceptualisation will be
able to identify within this programme (1) various *forms* of knowing, (2) different *orders* of knowing, (3) a *process of development* in
knowing and (4) the effect of *world-views* on knowing. *Looking at
Ourselves and Others* appears to address Bawden's plea for new
ways of thinking and knowing to be directed at troublesome
issues within interpersonal relationships.

Concluding Statement

During the lifetime of many of us, there have been unprecedented changes on this planet – the introduction of highly
sophisticated jet aeroplanes, television, radar, atom and hydro-
gen bombs, communications technology almost beyond imagination, new industrial materials, explorations of the universe,
aureomycin, penicillin, anti-polio vaccine and gene therapy, to
mention only some. All of these innovations, however, have been
in scientific and technological knowledge, and they serve to
highlight our lack of progress in other fields. As Toynbee (1989:
30) has said: 'The most alarming feature of present-day society is
that the power conferred by technology has recently increased to
an unprecedented degree at an unprecedented rate, while the
average level of the moral ... behavior of human beings who now
wield this vastly increased power has remained stationary, or
may actually have declined.'

The imbalance has arisen partly because of the relative difficulty of solving human relationship problems – tremendously
difficult though it is, it is probably much easier to land a person
on the moon than it is to have Israelis and Palestinians living
together peacefully on the West Bank, here on Earth. The other
cause of the imbalance is the relatively high value that societies
(especially Western ones) have placed on scientific and technological development. Taken together, these two 'causes' present
a formidable obstacle to 'peace on earth'. What is needed is a
re-structuring of political, social and educational priorities to

give a higher ranking to the nurturance of such values as *equitable treatment of all, care and compassion, empathy* and *co-operation.* Until we do that, we will all suffer, for our future in the global village is, indeed, a common one.

References

Amato, P. 1987. *Children in Australian Families: The Growth of Competence.* (Quoted in Henry 1999). Prentice-Hall: Sydney.

Arunpairojana, R. 1987. The Effect of Group Size and Learning Structures upon the Value Which Low-Achieving Students Ascribe to Their School Programs. Unpublished Ph.D. thesis, University of Queensland.

Berrell, M. 1993. Classrooms as the sites of citizenship education. In K. Kennedy *et al.* (eds.). *Citizenship Education for a New Age.* University of Southern Queensland Press: Toowoomba.

Berrell, M., and Gloet, M. 1995. *Computer and Goal Structures: Improving Computer Use in Classrooms through Cooperative Approaches.* St Louis Press: Sydney.

Burbules, N.C. 1997. A grammar of difference: some ways of rethinking difference and diversity as educational topics. *Australian Educational Researcher,* vol. 24, no. 1.

Campbell, J. 1981. *The Quality and Teaching Costs of Alternative Arrangements Made for Rural Secondary-School Students in South-East Queensland.* Report to Educational Research and Development Committee, Canberra.

————. 1990. Class-sizes revisited. *New Horizons in Education,* no. 83.

Campbell, J., and McMeniman, M. 1983. *A Comparative Study of Alternative and Mainstream Courses at Year 11.* Australian Government Publishing Service: Canberra.

Campbell, J., McMeniman, M.M. and Baikaloff, N. 1992. *Visions of a Future Australian Society: Towards an Educational Curriculum for 2000 AD and Beyond.* Ministerial Consultative Council on Curriculum: Brisbane.

Coleman, J.S., *et al.* 1966. *Equality of Educational Opportunity.* Office of Education, U.S. Department of Health, Education and Welfare: Washington, DC.

Eckersley, R. 1990. Casualties of Change to Agents of Change? Address to Australian Association for Adolescent Health, Perth.

Erikson, E.H. 1950. *Childhood and Society.* Norton: New York.

Graves, N. 1988. Education for a caring community? *New Era in Education*, vol. 69, no. 2.

Henry, M.B. 1996. *Young Children, Parents and Professionals*. Routledge: London.

———. 1999. Open doors, open minds: innovative courses in 'working with parents and community'. In N.J. Yelland (ed.). *Innovations in Practice: Promoting Meaningful Learning for Early Childhood Professionals*. National Association for the Education of Young Children: Washington, DC.

Hess, R.D. 1971. Community involvement in day care. *Day Care: Resources for Decisions*. (Quoted in Henry 1999) U.S. Office of Economic Opportunity: Washington, DC.

Hill, B. V. 1992. Values education in State schools. *New Horizons in Education*, no. 87.

Michael, T. 1999. Bullying in Early Childhood Settings: The Causes and the Cure. Conference paper, Brisbane.

Northey, D. 1990. Exploring Pacific issues through small-group cooperative learning. In D. Wilson *et al.* (eds.). *Asia and the Pacific – Issues of Educational Policy, Curriculum and Practice*. Detselig: Calgary.

Oats, W.N. 1986. *Headmaster by Chance*. Aguerremendi Press: Hobart.

Ochiltree, G., and Edgar, D. 1995. *Today's Child Care, Tomorrow's Children!* (Quoted in Henry 1999) Australian Institute of Family Studies: Melbourne.

Passmore, J. 1985. Educating for the twenty-first century. *Quadrant* (August).

Porter, P. 1997. Knowledge, skills and compassion? *Australian Education Researcher*, vol. 24, no. 1.

Ramsay, P., Sneddon, D., Grenfell, J. and Ford, I. 1983. Successful and unsuccessful schools: a study in southern Auckland. *Australian and New Zealand Journal of Sociology*, vol. 19, no. 2.

Sharan, S. 1980. Cooperative learning in small groups: recent methods and effects on achievement, attitudes and ethnic relations. *Review of Education Research*, vol. 50, no. 2.

Skilbeck, M. 1988. Caring in action: foreword. *New Horizons in Education*, no. 79.

Slavin, R. 1983. When does cooperative learning increase student achievement? *Psychological Bulletin*, vol. 94, no. 3.

Slee, P., and Rigby, K. 1991. Victims and Bullies in the School Setting. Conference Proceedings of the Australian Guidance and Counselling Association, Melbourne.

Toynbee, A. 1989. Good and evil. In R.L. Gage (ed.). *Choose Life: A Dialogue*. Oxford University Press: Oxford.

UNESCO. 1989. *International Symposium and Round Table*. Final Report. UNESCO Publishing: Paris.

US Peace Corps/World Wise Schools Program. 1993. *Looking at Ourselves and Others*. US Peace Corps: Washington, D.C.

Valadian, M. 1999. Teaching with Care: Learners Will Care. Address to 40th International Conference of WEF, Launceston.

Walter, J. 1990. *City, Family and Nation: Visions for a New Australia*. Griffith University Press: Brisbane.

Woolman, D.C. 1999. Schooling for Civility: Conflict Resolution Programs as a Response to Youth Violence. Paper presented at 40th International Conference of WEF, Launceston.

Eight

EDUCATING FOR A SUSTAINABLE FUTURE

John Fien

Sustainable Development: A Holistic Concept

Most people in the world today have an immediate and intuitive sense of the need to build a sustainable future. They may not be able to provide a precise definition of 'sustainable development' or 'sustainability' – indeed, even experts debate that issue – but they clearly sense the danger and the need for informed action. They smell the problem in the air, they taste it in their water; they see it in more congested living spaces and blemished landscapes; they read about it in the newspapers and hear about it on radio and television.... Both opinion polls and casual conversations suggest that people are increasingly beginning to sense that something has gone seriously wrong, that there must be some connection among the growing difficulties they encounter and read about, even if they cannot provide an adequate explanation of exactly what it is or how it has developed. (UNESCO-EPD 1997: 7)

Although, as the above quotation states, there is still debate about the precise definition of 'sustainable development', there is growing acceptance that it is a process by which one group of people's use of environments and resources does not jeopardise the environments and well-being of others, or destroy the capacities of future generations to satisfy their reasonable needs and wants. The scenario is changing from one in which 'long-haired greenies, determined to impede progress' wage battle with 'greedy developers hell-bent on destroying our heritage', to one in which people with legitimate conflicting interests acknowledge that survival in the only environment available to us requires compromise from all. In the words of David Yencken, the former President of the Australian Conservation Foundation, 'Sustainable development is an inspired way in which a bridge can be built between two conflicting paradigms, between the paradigm that has underlain past Western approaches to the environment and an emerging new environmental paradigm' (1994: 221).

That sustainable development is not currently in evidence is suggested by atmospheric warming and climatic change, the destruction of rainforests and threats to biodiversity, accelerating rates of land degradation and desertification, population-resource imbalances, urban decay, nuclear accidents, the disposal of toxic wastes and a range of other threats to the quality of human life and the sustainability of ecosystems. There are also rising levels of concern about the problems associated with global inequalities in standards of living and human well-being: regional conflicts; great imbalances in the consumption of resources between countries and regions; droughts and famines; the increasing marginalisation of women, ethnic minorities, indigenous peoples, the unemployed and the physically disabled; accumulating foreign debt; the failure of the world to solve the trade and transport problems that still cause hunger and malnutrition; and the necessity for many people to overexploit the resources of their local environment for daily survival. These all reflect a situation of *un*sustainability – one in which the present use of environments and resources by some *is* jeopardising the environments and well-being of others, and *is* destroying the capacities of future generations to satisfy their reasonable needs and wants.

It is important to note two things about the situation presented above. *Firstly*, the seemingly disparate issues and problems are not unrelated. As the World Commission on Environment and Development (1987: 4) states:

Until recently, the planet was a large world in which human activities and their effects were neatly compartmentalized within nations ... and within broad areas of concern (environmental, economic, social). These compartments have begun to dissolve. This applies in particular to the various global 'crises' that have seized public concern, particularly over the last decade. These are not separate crises: an environmental crisis, a development crisis, an energy crisis. They are all one.

The Commissioners reported that this realisation made them focus on one theme – that many present development trends leave increasing numbers of people poor and vulnerable, and at the same time degrade the natural environment. As Elizabeth Dodswell, the former Executive Director of the United Nations Environmental Programme (UNEP), has stated (1995: 2):

> One point is of pivotal significance. No long-term strategy of poverty alleviation can succeed in the face of environmental forces that promote persistent erosion of the natural resources upon which we all depend. And no environmental protection programme can make headway without removing the day-to-day pressures of poverty that leave people little choice but to discount the future so deeply that they fail to protect the resource base necessary for their own survival and their children's well-being.

Secondly, these problems of unsustainability should not be regarded as ones requiring technical solutions, but rather as symptoms, or consequences, of the wider malaise of many of the modernist values and practices that have supplanted indigenous systems of sustainability and have put the world on its present unsustainable path. Thus, UNESCO-EPD (1997: 14) states:

> Sustainable development is as much an ethical precept as a scientific concept, as concerned with notions of equity as with theories of global warming. Sustainable development is widely understood to involve the natural sciences and economics, but it is even more fundamentally concerned with culture: with the values people hold and how they perceive their relations with others. It responds to an imperative need to imagine a new basis of relationships among peoples and with the habitat that sustains human life.

As these quotations suggest, instead of viewing the environment as nature and natural systems alone, we are coming to see it in a holistic sense as the totality of our surroundings and existence which results from the way we use nature and its resources to satisfy our needs and wants. This means seeing the environment as a complex web of global social, cultural, economic and political, as well as geo- and bio-physical, components. It also means realising that environmental and development problems cannot be understood without reference to social, economic and political values, and that managing the global crisis will depend upon changes in personal values, lifestyle choices, and global patterns of development and trade.

To help bring about changes in social and economic thinking, practices and institutions that can promote sustainable development, Schleicher (1989: 277–8) writes of the need for a new 'ecological ethic,… an ecologically oriented value system' based upon 'fundamental changes in human attitudes and actions towards ourselves and the environment'. The scope of such a change in social values has been likened to a change in social paradigms or world-views. This would involve a process of change towards social systems, institutions and practices guided by values such as empathy with other species, other people and future generations; respect for natural and social limits to growth; support for careful planning in order to minimise threats to nature and the quality of life; and a desire for a change in the way most societies conduct their economic and political affairs (Milbrath 1989).

The Role of Education

While there is debate about particular directions, the pace of the 'paradigm shift' referred to earlier and the effectiveness of different strategies for social change, there is wide agreement, both in Australia and internationally, that education has an important role to play in achieving sustainable development (Australian Department of the Environment and Heritage 1999). Unfortunately, much current practice in environmental education looks to individual behavioural change (i.e. more recycling and use of public transport, and less wasting of water and energy) as its ultimate goal. For sustainable development to be realised, however, it has to be recognised that environmental problems are structurally anchored in society and our ways of living, and that answers to them need to be sought in working to transform the social conditions of human and non-human life as well as individual lifestyles (Jensen and Schnack 1997). This draws attention to the economic and political structures, to poverty and other forms of social injustice, which cause and perpetuate unsustainable practices, and to a need to learn the processes by which such unsustainable practices can be eliminated through political processes. All of the major international environmental reports of recent years (IUCN, UNEP and WWFN 1991; United Nations Conference on Environment and Development 1992; World Commission on Environment and Development 1987) have stressed that the role of education is to help students to reflect critically on their place in the environment and to consider what sustainability means to them and their communities. It also involves practice in envisioning alternative ways of development and living, evaluating alternative visions, learning how to negotiate and justify choices between visions and making plans for achieving desired ones, and participating in community actions to bring such visions into effect. These all add up to what Jensen and Schnack (1997) call 'action competence' or 'environmental citizenship'. Action competence aligns education for sustainability as part of the process of building an informed, concerned and active civil society. As Orr argues (1992: 84), 'I see no prospect whatsoever for building a sustainable society without an active, engaged, informed, and competent citizenry'; he maintains that this requires 'an unwavering commitment by educational institutions to foster widespread civic competence'.

This case for active environmental citizenship as a goal of education means that educating for a sustainable future does not focus on direct problem solving *per se*. Rather, its focus is on the ways students learn to make judgements about when, how and why to work on their own, and with others, to help build sustainability from the local level upwards. As Schnack (1996: 11) argues:

> It is not and cannot be the task of the school to solve the political problems of society. It is not the task to improve the world with the help of the pupils' activities. These must be assessed on the basis of their formative value and thus according to educational criteria. A school, regarded as a school, does not become 'green' by conserving energy, collecting batteries or sorting waste. The crucial factor must be what the pupils are learning from participating in such activities.

Some Significant Facets of Education

In several of the earlier chapters of this book, it is implied that decisions which are made about national priorities, educational goals, educational objectives, curriculum, pedagogy, assessment and the like all have the potential to determine the kind of society that will be created. Since national priorities have an overarching, pervasive influence, it is useful to begin with a consideration of these in relation to educating for sustainability.

National Priorities

It is widely acknowledged that present-day governments have multiple, and sometimes contradictory, roles, and that these are manifested in diverse ways in educational policies and practices (Carnoy and Levin 1985; Schlechty 1990). For example, on the one hand, governments need to ensure that education systems socialise and educate citizens in ways that will enable them to contribute to desired economic activities and goals. This includes not only vocational knowledge and skills but also attitudes of responsibility, diligence, punctuality and social cohesion that will maintain and promote these goals. This is the 'reproductive' role of the State and education. On the other hand, particularly in democratic countries, governments need to take action to maintain their public legitimacy by anticipating trends that may challenge national well-being and by responding to public concerns about social problems, such as racism, poverty, public safety and, increasingly, the environment. Formal education is one way by which governments seek to achieve this goal, and this involves developing educational policies which enhance the capacities of citizens to respond to these anticipated challenges, to identify and articulate their concerns, and to contribute as active and informed citizens to solutions by participating in discussions about them and other public issues. This is the role of the State and education in 'constructing civil society'.

The curriculum is a product of both the 'reproductive' and the 'constructing civil society' roles of governments. Unfortunately, the press of short-term political and economic priorities often has given ascendancy to the reproductive roles of formal education. This situation of unbalanced priorities calls for a re-affirmation of the role of formal education in building civil society by helping students (1) develop criteria for determining what is best to conserve in their cultural, economic and natural heritage; (2) discern values and strategies for creating sustainability in their local communities; and (3) contribute their understanding, with that of others, to national and global issues. This is the contemporary version of what Dewey (1916) called the 'reconstructionist' tradition in education.

Goals and Objectives

Most countries in the world can point to ways in which their education systems are being re-oriented towards sustainability as a result of the expansion of scientific knowledge of the environment and growing public awareness of the increasing scale and severity of environmental problems. Most initiatives, however, have tended to come from departments of environment and heritage, agriculture or natural resources, rather than departments of education, with the consequence that they have sometimes remained embedded within pre–Earth Summit conceptions of environmental education, which have tended to favour science and conservation approaches rather than the holistic imperatives of education for sustainability. They have tended, also, to concentrate upon raising awareness and information campaigns, and to be directed at individual behavioural change, rather than broader educational goals. Nevertheless, in recent years there have been a number of attempts to suggest goals, objectives and guiding principles of education so that sustainable development may be enhanced. Many of these attempts have their origins in the Tbilisi Declaration (Intergovernmental Conference on Environmental Education 1977), which received wide and enduring international acceptance. Its long-term goals include (1) to foster awareness of, and concern about, the interdependence of natural, social, economic and political systems at local, national, regional and global levels; (2) to develop the knowledge, skills, values and ethical discernment and motivation to participate as an informed and active member of civil society; and (3) to encourage critical reflection and decision-making in the choice of personal lifestyle and civic participation in order to contribute to sustainable development (British Environment, Development, Education and Training Group 1992: 2).

Five interrelated categories of objectives contribute to these goals:

1. *Awareness:* To help individuals, groups and societies acquire an awareness and sensitivity to the interdependence of natural, social, economic and political systems, especially related to questions, issues and problems arising from the processes of sustainable development.
2. *Knowledge:* To help individuals, groups and societies gain a variety of experiences in, and a basic understanding of, the knowledge and action competencies required for sustainable development.
3. *Values:* To help individuals, groups and societies acquire feelings of concern for issues of sustainability as well as a set

of values upon which they can make judgements about appropriate ways of acting individually and with others to promote sustainable development.

4. *Skills:* To help individuals, groups and societies acquire the action competence – or skills of environmental citizenship – in order to be able to identify and anticipate environmental problems, and work with others to resolve, minimise and prevent them.

5. *Participation:* To provide individuals, groups and societies with opportunities to be actively involved in exercising their skills of environmental citizenship and be actively involved at all levels in working towards sustainable development.

Curriculum

Eco-feminist writers have identified the patriarchal assumptions and attitudes towards nature, women and development upon which modernist science is based as a major cause of environmental exploitation, poverty, and the increasing marginalisation of many of the world's people (Merchant 1980; Shiva 1985). Re-orienting education towards sustainability requires viewing science in a new way – as eco-science, which integrates action for sustainability with the interests of women and marginalised people. As Vandana Shiva argues (1989: xvii–xviii):

> A science that does not respect nature's needs and a development that does not respect people's needs inevitably threaten survival. In their fight to survive the onslaughts of both, women have begun a struggle that challenges the most fundamental categories of Western patriarchy – its concepts of nature and women, and of science and development. Their ecological struggles are aimed simultaneously at liberating nature from ceaseless exploitation and themselves from marginalisation. They are creating a feminist ideology that transcends gender, and a political practice that is humanly inclusive; they are challenging patriarchy's ideological claim to universalism not with another universalising tendency, but with diversity; and they are challenging the dominant concept of power as violence with the alternative of non-violence as power.

Viewed from this perspective, education for sustainability reflects an alternative epistemology to that of modernist science and seeks to educate young people to value diverse ways of knowing, to identify with their own cultural heritage and value it as a contribution to the global cultural diversity, and to respect community-based approaches to social change. Such an epistemology also helps to redress the dominance of natural science and nature study in much contemporary environmental education. The natural sciences provide important abstract knowledge of the world but, of themselves, do not contribute to sustainable development. Indeed, education in modernist ways of science has proven to be a recurring means through which mal-development has occurred. Hence, an important aspect of re-orienting formal education towards sustainability will be the development of interdisciplinary curricula which successfully impart scientific and technological knowledge while, simultaneously, emphasising the essentially social nature of decisions about how such knowledge is used.

Focusing upon the concepts that underlie sustainable development, within the context of seeking solutions to real problems that confront us, can help to ensure that education contributes to student learning that is holistic, has a moral base, and is integrated. As the 1989 UNESCO Report states (5):

> Our education system has suffered from the increased fragmentation of knowledge into often meaningless and irrelevant units. We need a new approach to knowledge which is more integrated. This integrated approach can probably best be realised by focussing knowledge on seeking the solutions to real problems which face us at all levels from the local to the global.

Among the 'real problems' that could be expected to feature in the curriculum (Fien 1995; adapted from Beddis and Johnson 1988) are:

• There are great differences in the availability and use of resources around the world, with poverty and need in some areas matched by overproduction and overconsumption in others. *How can the overconsumption, waste and misuse of resources by some people be reduced? How can the severe poverty that causes many to exploit the earth just to survive be eliminated? How can the pressure on the environment from both causes be overcome?*
• Some economic activities do great harm to environments, resources and communities. *How can economic activity be*

made of benefit to the communities and the companies involved, and without critical damage to the environment?

- Economic growth in some parts of the world is so high that it is leading to the production and consumption of many items that are super-luxuries and use resources that could otherwise be used to satisfy the needs of many of the world's poor. *How can the resources consumed by such luxuries be re-directed to aid the poor or be conserved for future generations?*

- Relatively high population densities and growth rates in certain parts of the world and the associated pressure on the local resource base are symptoms of the legacy of colonialism and present-day structural inequalities in the world economic system rather than causes of environmental problems. Appropriate social development lies at the heart of the solution to population and environmental pressures. *How can the nexus between the environment, social development and population growth be formulated to ensure the sustainable use of resources?*

- The indigenous and farming peoples of many countries have developed an ethic of sustainability and associated land use practices that have preserved their culture and harmony between people and nature for millennia. *How can the rights of these people be maintained and the knowledge and wisdom they possess be shared with others in all parts of the world?*

- Women and young people have a vital role to play in environmental care and development, now and into the future. They have viewpoints, skills and interests that can help maximise the potential for sustainable development. *How can the wisdom, courage and talents of women and young people be used as a model for sustainable development policies and practices?*

- The most effective arena for action on sustainability and justice issues is the local community. *How can people best organise themselves locally – and liaise with others nationally and globally – to collaborate in the movement towards sustainable development?*

Within the context of problems such as those above, eight concepts for guiding teaching and learning are suggested below. These are adapted from concepts in the 1991 ICUN, UNEP and WWFN report, *Caring for the Earth*, and may be categorised into two groups – those related to human responsibility to care for nature (ecological sustainability), and those related to our responsibility to care for each other (social justice).

People and Nature: Ecological Sustainability

1. *Interdependence:* People are part of natural systems and depend utterly on them. Thus, natural systems should be respected at all times. To respect natural systems means to approach nature with humility, care and compassion; to be frugal and efficient in resource use; to be guided by the best available knowledge, both traditional and scientific; and to help shape and support public policies that promote sustainability.
2. *Biodiversity:* Every life form warrants respect and preservation independently of its worth to people. People should preserve the complexity of ecosystems to ensure the survival of all species and the safeguarding of their habitats and, through this, contribute also to the material and spiritual quality of human life.
3. *Living lightly:* All people should take responsibility for their impact on natural systems. They should not interfere unduly with ecological processes, diminish diversity, or overexploit renewable resources and the ecosystems that support them. They should use natural resources and the environment carefully and sustainably, and restore degraded ecosystems.
4. *Interspecies equity:* People should treat all creatures decently, and protect them from cruelty and avoidable suffering.

People and People: Social Justice

5. *Basic human needs:* The needs of all individuals and societies should be met, within the constraints imposed by the biosphere, and all should have equal opportunity for improving their lot.
6. *Intergenerational equity:* Each generation should leave to the future a world that is at least as diverse and productive as the one it inherited. To this end, non-renewable resources should be used sparingly, renewable resources should be used sustainably, and waste should be minimised. The benefits of development should not be consumed now if the costs are left to the future.
7. *Human rights:* All people should have the fundamental freedoms of conscience and religion, expression, peaceful assembly and association.

8. *Democracy:* All people and communities should be empowered to exercise responsibility for their own lives and for life on earth. Thus they must have full access to education, political enfranchisement and sustaining livelihoods. They should also be able to participate effectively in the decisions that most affect them.

These eight concepts can be seen as principles or values that underlie images of a sustainable future. Four of these images are: (1) a fair, equal and just future, (2) a safe and peaceful future, (3) an ecologically sustainable future and (4) a democratic future. Images or visions of the future are continuously being promoted by business, advertising and politicians, and in the media and science fiction. They play a critical role in the creation of change, as well as affecting what we think is worth doing in the present. An excellent example of the creative power generated by images, especially when shared with others, is given by Colin N. Power in Chapter 2 of this volume, in which he reports on the outcomes of the 1990 UNESCO-sponsored World Conference on Education for All held in Jomtien, Thailand. Obviously, we can most easily work towards our preferred future if we have clear images of where we want to go and how we might get there. As Elise Boulding (1988) writes:

> At any moment, there are hundreds of images of possible futures being generated within each society, and thousands for the planet as a whole. In any cultural epoch, only certain images of the future out of that much wider pool develop enough cultural resonance to affect the course of events. There is selective empowerment of certain images, which 'explode' later, like time bombs, into the realised future.

A crisis of direction in society, national or global, may stimulate the emergence of new guiding images, and in this present period of rapid change and social upheaval, it may well be that the concept of sustainability provides such an image. Box 1 (see page 134) is a sample teaching activity that may be used to explore images of a sustainable future.

Pedagogy

In the opinion of many, choices of teaching and learning strategies are the most significant determinants of the learning experiences of students and the nature of the objectives achieved, irrespective of whatever sustainable development themes and

---

BOX 1: Envisioning a Sustainable Future

Consider each of the following images of a sustainable future, in turn, and answer the following four questions pertaining to it:

Why is this a critical image for a sustainable future?
What might it *look like* in practice?
What is *already* being done to bring this image into reality, and by whom?
What role would you like to play in helping bring this image into reality? Why?

1. A fair, equal and just future
What one 'has' should not depend on who one 'is' in society. Thus the practices and procedures for allocating resources should not discriminate, directly or indirectly, on the basis of gender, race, class, culture or group. Everyone should have access to the basic necessities of life such as food, clothes, shelter, health care and education. There should be both a minimum level of welfare, below which no one should drop, and, due to the finite nature of the earth's resources, a maximum level, beyond which no one should exceed.

2. A safe and peaceful future
No one should be subjected to direct personal violence, e.g. through assault, robbery or war, and neither should they suffer from indirect violence. Unjust social, political and economic systems can equally cause suffering in the form of poverty, hunger and other deprivation.

3. An ecologically sustainable future
This requires full and appropriate protection of the biosphere on which all life depends. Thus the rights of non-human species must be recognised, as well as the need for concerned stewardship of air, water, soil, creatures and plants.

4. A democratic future
Genuine participation in all aspects of one's own life offers opportunities for responsibility, personal growth and enrichment. It means being in control of one's own life choices and being free to choose. This leads to ownership of decisions and is the reverse of alienation.

topics or curriculum structures are adopted. Whitty (1985), for example, claims that whether or not particular curriculum plans are ultimately reproductive or transformative (i.e. contributing to empowerment for participation in civil society) is essentially a matter of how they are worked on pedagogically and how they are articulated with other issues in and beyond the school. Similarly, Evans states (1993: 25): 'The way forward in education may not lie in radical macro curriculum innovation, but in a much more thorough analysis of micro learning and teaching settings, practices and experiences – particularly if this is done with an eye to increasing the real sense of success and control experienced by all students.' Issues of pedagogy are vital in the re-orientation of education towards sustainability.

The reconstructionist tradition in education, which is espoused in this chapter, involves two related processes: first, what has been discussed above, namely, the organisation of knowledge around a range of significant real problems and concepts, so that students can become critical thinkers, and, second, the participation of students in community affairs, so that they might become active members of civil society.

Viewing pedagogy as a process of encouraging students to explore questions, issues and problems of sustainability, especially in contexts relevant to them and their communities, means that student-centred and interactive enquiry-based approaches to teaching and learning need to be seen as central aspects of pedagogy in education for sustainability. Such approaches do not preclude the use of more teacher-centred methods such as exposition, narration and demonstration when appropriate. It does mean, however, that, whenever possible, student learning will be based in the community, will use the environment and community as a resource for learning, and will involve such activities as debating controversial issues, role play, simulation games, values clarification and analysis, and discovery learning, as well as a range of creative and experiential activities (Fien, Heck and Ferreira 1997). Naish, Rawling and Hart (1986: 46) identify the characteristics of such an enquiry-based pedagogy by describing it as an approach to teaching and learning which:

- identifies questions, issues and problems as the starting point for enquiry;
- involves students as active participants in a sequence of meaningful learning;

- provides opportunities for the development of a wide range of skills and abilities (intellectual, social, practical and communication);
- presents opportunities for fieldwork and classroom work to be closely integrated;
- provides possibilities for open-ended enquiries in which attitudes and values may be clarified and an open interchange of ideas and opinions can take place;
- provides scope for an effective balance of both teacher-directed work and more independent student enquiry;
- assists in the development of political literacy such that students gain understanding of the social world and how to participate in it.

Strategic Questioning is an innovative teaching strategy that reflects these principles of enquiry-based pedagogy, and Box 2 is an introduction to the process.

Box 2: Strategic Questioning

Individuals, families and communities are best placed to tackle global issues at the local level – and it is at the local level that teachers, schools and students can also learn skills for building a sustainable future.

The first step in learning such skills is to be able to ask the right sort of questions – questions that will lead to an action plan for change. Strategic Questioning is a valuable technique for this process.

Strategic Questioning is a form of thinking about change. It was developed by Fran Peavy, a social change worker from North America. Change is often accompanied by a range of uncomfortable emotions, including denial, fear and resistance. However, change also provides opportunities for new ideas to emerge. Strategic Questioning assists the integration of new ideas and strategies into the development of communities in such a way that people can feel comfortable.

Six 'families' of questions are used in Strategic Questioning. These move from introductory documentation questions through to more dynamic and reflective questions. These question families are:

- Observation Questions
- Feelings/Affective Questions

- Visioning Questions
- Change Questions
- Personal Inventory and Support Questions
- Personal Action Questions

Strategic Questioning helps people create their own solutions to their own problems. For example, Strategic Questioning has been used in India by communities as a means of identifying strategies for improving water quality in the Ganges River. Local people, in partnership with the government, are developing exciting new ways to clean up the river for themselves and their children.

One of the assumptions behind the Strategic Questioning process is that questions have the potential to be significant. This activity is based upon a set of the six families and a range of 'prompt questions' for each one.

In Strategic Questioning, people usually work in pairs, one as a 'speaker' and one as a 'listener', to discuss a theme.

1. To begin, find a partner and decide who will be the 'speaker' and who will be the 'listener'.
2. The 'speaker' selects a local issue that he or she is most concerned about. It is important to state the issue in terms of a real, tangible local problem that actually concerns you and others in your community, rather than an abstract or theoretical problem.

   For example:

   Too general: 'I am concerned about the future of young people.'

   Specific: 'I am concerned about the future of young people in my city who seem unable to find a job after school.'

   Too general: 'I am concerned about too many trees being cut down around the world.'

   Specific: 'I am concerned about the council's plans to cut down the trees along Catilla Road in order to widen it into a four-lane highway.'

3. The 'listener' then asks the following set of questions in conversational style, using the prompt questions when they might be helpful.

   Observation Questions
   - What is the issue that concerns you now?
   - What are the three main things you know about it?

(continued on next page)

Box 2: Strategic Questioning *(continued)*

- How did you learn these things?
- Is this information you can trust?

Feelings/Affective Questions

- How do you feel about this topic/issue?
- How has this issue affected your own physical or emotional health (that you know of)?
- What sensations do you feel in your body when you think or talk about this topic/issue?

Visioning Questions

- What is the meaning of this issue in your own life?
- How could this issue be addressed/changed so that it would be as you wish it to be?

Change Questions

- What will it take to bring the current situation towards the ideal?
- What exactly needs to change here?
- How might these changes come about? Name as many ways as possible.

Personal Inventory and Support Questions

- What would it take for you to participate in the change?
- What would you like to do that might be useful in bringing about these changes?
- What support would you need to work for this change?

Personal Action Questions

- Whom do you need to talk to?
- How can you get others to a meeting to work on this issue?

4. Analyse your experience of Strategic Questioning by answering the following questions.
   - What do you think of the Strategic Questioning process?
   - Do you feel that it is an authentic way of communicating? Why or why not?
   - Does the process help you feel any more confident about the future?
   - Do you feel a little better prepared to engage in action, having participated in the Strategic Questioning process?
   - How could the Strategic Questioning process be incorporated into your teaching?

Primacy is given to the regular involvement of students in developing and evaluating visions of alternative futures, learning how to resolve problems, and actively working in and with the community on problems that are of significance to them. These three aspects of action-focused pedagogy emphasise the importance of actively involving students in projects to build sustainability in their local communities. Without regular experiences such as these, the re-orientation of objectives, curriculum themes, concepts and course structures for sustainability will be in vain. Empowerment to work for sustainability is the *raison d'être* of re-orienting formal education towards sustainability.

One of the participants in the Campbell, McMeniman and Baikaloff study (1992) wrote: 'Maitland, an English constitutional historian, proclaimed a century ago that history was a seamless web. That is the message that education should proclaim, substituting "knowledge" for "history."' An interesting example of how a classroom teacher can re-structure the curriculum into something approaching that 'seamless web', and, at the same time, extend a constructive local experience into regional and even international ones is revealed in this delightful excerpt from a paper prepared by Helen Cameron (1999) for the Launceston 40th International Conference of WEF.

Adopt-a-Farm

People often ask me what I teach. I used to think about it a bit – what do you say? 'Maths, English, Social Science. Whatever they give me!' These days I say, 'Environmental Science', because that's what it is! When my principal approached me three years ago to ask if I would be the school guinea pig and help them out of a fix by taking one grade-seven class for four subjects, a revolutionary change occurred in my teaching – four subjects from textbooks? No way! It had to be hands on. That's how I got into the Adopt-a-Farm program.

Adopt-a-Farm provides education for sustainable living. The students learn about problem conditions on the farm through conducting soil tests, water tests and earthworm counts; releasing dung beetles; collecting local native seeds; propagating; and planting out shelter belts. They learn about the importance of diversity on the farm and the benefits of maintaining native forest on the land. They learn how to go about solving real problems.

Students also learn to think beyond their local environment by learning about the issues of their own area and then transferring them to a wider picture. My adopted farm has frog ponds, and our final visit for the year was a frog night. Of course, the students were tuned into the significance of declining frog numbers world wide.

One of the main aims of Adopt-a-Farm is to act as a way of linking the urban and rural communities, in order to provide urban students (and their families) with an understanding of what farms are all about and where our food comes from. Students have found all this fascinating, and are happy to adopt the farmers along with the farm, and, of course, the dog comes, too!

One of the offshoots of Adopt-a-Farm for me is a programme called Science across Asia/Pacific. Students conduct a survey in their own community – in our case, we are looking at energy – and send off their findings internationally via the Internet. When they receive results from other students, there is a lot of scope for learning about the lifestyles of people elsewhere and for opening up dialogue on related themes. Students begin to empathise with those less well off than themselves.

Conclusion

Re-orienting education towards sustainability is a process of educational reform and innovation. It is possible that pre–Earth Summit forms of education could be considered a 'failed innovation', despite the initiatives that could be cited. As Fullan with Stiegelbauer (1991: 354) laments: 'We have a huge negative legacy of failed reform that cannot be overcome simply through good intentions and powerful rhetoric.' Re-orienting environmental education for sustainability is powerful rhetoric and a great intention. We have much to learn, however, about the processes of educational innovation and change. Learning from the successful experiences of other educational reform movements, and interpreting their lessons to education for sustainability and local cultural and educational contexts, must become the new priority of priorities for environmental education. As Orr (1992: 83, 145) states, the crisis of sustainability – the fit between humanity and its habitat – must be viewed not only as a permanent feature on the public agenda, but as *the* agenda. He concludes:

> No other issue of politics, economics and public policy will remain unaffected by the crisis of resources, population, climate change, species extinction, acid rain, deforestation, ozone depletion, and soil loss. Sustainability is about the terms and conditions of human survival.... Those presuming to educate should not stand aloof from the

decisions about how and whether life will be lived in the twenty-first century. To do so would be to miss the Mount Everest issues on the historical topography of our age, and condemn ourselves to irrelevance.

As Colin N. Power states in Chapter 2, 'The challenges are great, and the stakes are high.'

References

Australian Department of the Environment and Heritage. 1999. *Today Shapes Tomorrow: Environment Education for a Sustainable Future.* Canberra.

Beddis, R., and Johnson, C. 1988. *Only One Earth: A Multi-Media Education Pack.* World Wide Fund for Nature: Godalming.

Boulding, E. 1988. *Building a Global Civic Culture.* Teachers College Press: New York.

British Environment, Development, Education and Training Group. 1992. *Good Earth-Keeping: Education, Training and Awareness for a Sustainable Future.* Sterling, UK.

Cameron, H. 1999. Adopt-a-Farm. Paper presented at the 40th International Conference of WEF, Launceston.

Campbell, J., McMeniman, M.M. and Baikaloff, N. 1992. *Visions of a Future Australian Society: Towards an Educational Curriculum for 2000 AD and Beyond.* Ministerial Consultative Council on Curriculum: Brisbane.

Carnoy, M., and Levin, H. 1985. *Schooling and Work in the Democratic State.* Stanford University Press: Stanford.

Dewey, J. 1916. *Democracy and Education.* Macmillan: New York.

Dodswell, E. 1995. *Our Planet.* United Nations Environmental Programme: Paris.

Evans, G. 1993. Windows on education: a skills-referenced perspective. *New Horizons in Education,* vol. 88.

Fien, J. (ed.). 1995. *Teaching for a Sustainable World.* UNESCO-UNEP International Environmental Education Programme for Teacher Education. Griffith University, Brisbane.

Fien, J., Heck, D. and Ferreira, J. (eds.). 1997. *Learning for a Sustainable Environment: A Workshop Manual for Teacher Educators.* UNESCO-ACEID: Bangkok.

Fullan, M., with Stiegelbauer, S. 1991. *The New Meaning of Educational Change.* Cassell Educational Limited: London.

Intergovernmental Conference on Environmental Education. 1977. *Tbilisi Declaration.* UNESCO Publishing: Paris.

IUCN, UNEP and WWFN. 1991. *Caring for the Earth*. IUCN: Gland.

Jensen, B.B., and Schnack, K. 1997. The action competence approach in environmental education. *Environmental Education Research*, vol. 3, no. 2, 163–78.

Merchant, C. 1980. *The Death of Nature: Women, Ecology and the Scientific Revolution*. Harper and Row: San Francisco.

Milbrath, L. 1989. *Envisioning a Sustainable Society: Learning Our Way Out*. SUNY Press: Albany.

Naish, M., Rawling, E. and Hart, C. 1986. *Geography 16–19: The Contribution of a Curriculum Project to 16–19 Education*. Longman: Harlow.

Orr, D. 1992. *Ecological Literacy: Education and the Transition to a Postmodern World*. State University of New York Press: Albany.

Schlechty, P. 1990. *Schools for the 21st Century*. Jossey-Bass: San Francisco.

Schleicher, K. 1989. Beyond environmental education: the need for ecological awareness. *International Review of Education*, vol. 35, no. 3, 257–81.

Schnack, K. 1996. Internationalisation, democracy and environmental education. In S. Breiting and K. Nielsen (eds.). *Environmental Education Research in the Nordic Countries*. Proceedings of the Research Centre for Environmental and Health Education, no. 33. The Royal Danish School of Educational Studies, Copenhagen.

Shiva, V. 1989. *Staying Alive – Women, Ecology and Development*. Zed Books: London.

UNESCO. 1989. *International Symposium and Round Table*. Final Report. UNESCO Publishing: Paris.

UNESCO-EPD. 1997. Educating for a Sustainable Future: A Transdisciplinary Vision for Concerted Action. Background paper, International Conference, Environment and Society: Education and Public Awareness for Sustainability, Thassaloniki, 8–12, December.

United Nations Conference on Environment and Development. 1992. *Agenda 21*. UNESCO Publishing: Paris.

Whitty, G. 1985. *Sociology and School Knowledge: Curriculum Theory, Research and Politics*. Methuen: London.

World Commission on Environment and Development. 1987. *Our Common Future*. Oxford University Press: Oxford.

Yencken, D. 1994. Values, knowledge and action. In L. Grove, D. Evans and D. Yencken (eds.). *Restoring the Land: Environmental Values, Knowledge and Action*. Melbourne University Press: Melbourne.

— Nine —

A WEAVING OF THREADS

The Warp and the Weft of the WEF Project

Bruce Keepes and Jillian M. Maling

As the editor explains in the preface, this book is best regarded as Stage III of the WEF Project, building upon the previous two stages, the first of which is represented here by Chapter 3 and the second being a week-long international conference in Launceston. Four of the chapters are based on keynote addresses at the conference (Chapter 2, Power 1999; Chapter 5, Hill 1999; Chapter 6, Bawden 1999; Chapter 8, Fien 1999); four (Chapter 1, J. Campbell; Chapter 3, J. Campbell, McMeniman and Baikaloff; Chapter 4, Oats; Chapter 7, E. Campbell) were written especially for this volume by people who were deeply involved in both Stages I and II of the project but were not keynote speakers at the conference; and three of the conference addresses (de Bono 1999; McMeniman 1999; Valadian 1999), which gave inspirational leadership at Stage II, do not appear as chapters in this book, but are drawn upon freely by us here.

One of the features of the Stage II conference were group reflection sessions held at the end of each day in which participants went over the day's sessions, shared insights and identified issues they would like pursued further. We summarised those reports each day and have drawn on them in shaping this chapter. Thus, in 'A Weaving of Threads: The Warp and the Weft of the WEF Project', we draw on both Stage I and Stage II of the project.

Each of the threads that we have chosen to draw together overlaps and interacts with the others. Some are completely woven into the cloth, while others are just touched upon. The first group – the warp – focuses primarily on the vision, and included here are more detailed considerations of the *human spirit* (Oats, Chapter 4); *moral responsibility* (Hill, Chapter 5); *ways of thinking, knowing and learning* (Bawden, Chapter 6); *humane values* (E. Campbell, Chapter 7); and *global responsibilities and perspectives* (Power, Chapter 2; Fien, Chapter 8). These topics, as Chapter 3 reports, were drawn from the major issues identified in the 1992 Campbell, McMeniman and Baikaloff study.

In addition, there are many threads – the weft – related to moving the visions into action. They glint here and there in the fabric and, while not treated as fully as those emerging directly from Stage I, are recurrent. These include forms of education; the role that education can and should play; the role of teachers and teaching; the shape and selected elements of a curriculum for the twenty-first century; and the creation of a web of collaborative action which spans individuals, groups and organisations, as well as localities, regions and nations.

The Warp

The Human Spirit

Chapter 3 starts the process of tangling with a definition for the human spirit. It speaks of it as 'the essential nature of what it is to be human', an element in the human search for meaning, and in 'our explorations of the unknown and our glimpse of the unity and interrelatedness of all components of what we know as the universe'.

In Chapter 4, Oats admits the difficulty of definition, but has no difficulty in outlining two case-studies of schools which he sees as working to nurture the human spirit. In so doing, he echoes Campbell *et al.*'s suggestion that it relates to our search for meaning. He quotes Capra (1988) suggesting that it could be defined as 'a mode of consciousness in which we feel connected to the cosmos as a whole'. He goes on to say that the 'witness' to the human spirit lies more in the realm of metaphor and poetry than definition and dissertation, relying on 'its own intuitive powers of imagination to guide it through the surrounding darkness beyond the reach of reason's searchlight'. He supports Palmer's contention that, without it, teachers dispense 'facts at the expense of meaning, information at the expense of wisdom'. Oats stresses the importance, in learning, of opportunities being given for students (1) to become conscious that the world is an interrelated whole, (2) to develop faith in humanity and (3) to be able to set their views in relation to those of others. He thus confirms the close relationship between ways of knowing and the human spirit, but it is Bawden who asserts the 'inspirational' as a form of knowing. Note that the term 'knowing' is used rather than 'knowledge'. As Huebner (1985: 172) has said:

> The problem, of course, is that schools and other institutions of education are not places of knowing, but places of knowledge. Knowledge is the fallout from the knowing process. Knowledge is form separated from life. It stands by itself, removed from the vitality and dynamics of life, from the spirit. It becomes life only when it is brought again into the knowing process of an individual.

In Chapter 6, Bawden argues for the role of inspirational knowing in ascertaining what 'should' be done, aiming at meaningful, rather than just thoughtful, action. He suggests the vital importance of integrating inspirational insights with other forms of knowing, and explicitly connects this way of knowing with morality and ethics, placing it with the ethical concerns of 'innate' rights and duties. That, in turn, indicates the connection between what Bawden sees as a form of knowing and one of Power's recurrent themes: the right of each human being and each culture to be respected.

Moral Responsibility, Values and the Common Good

Although Hill, in Chapter 5, directly addresses these issues, they are – along with ways of knowing, care and compassion, and ecological responsibility – a thread that re-occurs in other forms and at other points of the Stage I/Stage II WEF Project. In various ways, all of the authors are concerned with the fragmentation of modern society, its tensions and conflicts, and with its perceived directions and uncertainties. Each, in different ways, argues for the importance of re-asserting the common good and particular values. It is, for example, a sustained theme of Elizabeth Campbell's Chapter 7.

Throughout Chapter 2, Power emphasises acting in ways that respect the dignity and worth of each person and each culture across the globe, arguing that we must aim for both global unity and individual cultural diversity: 'Unity in diversity is difficult, but it is the only option.' Fien stresses that *individual* behavioural changes in values and treatment of the environment on their own are not sufficient and need to be accompanied by changes in the world-views of communities. He argues that young people must be educated 'to value diverse ways of knowing, to identify with their own cultural heritage and value it as a contribution to the global cultural diversity, and to respect community-based approaches to social change'. Bawden also speaks of world-views. He suggests that maturity involves being able to hold different world-views in perspective at the same time: 'We are mature when we have learned not only how to appreciate different perspectives, but how to accommodate them, too.' He writes of communities as 'collections of people with significant differences between them, seeking to know how to adapt to the ever changing world about them collectively'. Elizabeth Campbell, using multiculturalism as an example, makes a similar point: teaching or learning about other cultures is not enough on its own. There must be engagement with the study of difference itself and the meaning of those differences for the learners themselves as well as other people.

How is the common good to be achieved? By working towards real maturity as both individuals and members of a community, Bawden might reply. Power argues that it is imperative to look for a 'core of shared ethical values and principles', and to establish a 'global ethics' with democracy, human rights, peace and pluralism as basic ingredients. He argues that '[o]ur vision and action must combine universalistic principles with cultural differences, and our debate must include and respect everybody – every cultural and social group, particularly those who are currently excluded'. He draws attention to UNESCO's *Universal Ethics Project* (1998), which indicates that there are several key values and principles valid across cultures, religions and societies. These include human rights as well as equity and self-determination. There is also wide agreement that concern for others, responsibility, good manners, tolerance and respect for other people are important values.

Hill argues that moral education must be pursued. It should be aimed at knowing about values, obligations and differences, and at acting – individually and collectively – in a morally responsible way and for the common good: 'It is a pervasive theme in the present book that human beings must be alerted to the dependence of their humanity on the quality of the moral choices they make on behalf of themselves and others.'

He argues that a consensus about which values to teach *can* be achieved, citing as an example the Western Australian Agreed Minimum Values Framework. He sets out how, despite the difficulties, schools and teachers can handle this area effectively, especially when working with the communities in which they are located and with the 'third partner' – voluntary youth organisations.

Hill goes on to offer a set of guidelines for moral education, including the development of ways of talking about values; negotiating core values; identifying agreed values, rights and goals; celebrating diversity; and educating for better people. Those guidelines, along with those given in Chapter 7, are, themselves, instances of bold educational policies which, he argues, are required if moral education is to be an integral part of learning, teaching and doing.

Ways of Thinking, Knowing and Learning

Some authors in this book speak of thinking, some of knowing and others of learning. More than one links these concepts together, as we have chosen to do here and as participants in Stage II also did.

During Stage II of the WEF Project, de Bono spoke about new ways of thinking and knowing, as did Bawden in his keynote address, 'Learning to Lay Down the Path Walking', and in Chapter 6 of this book. Both share a sense of urgency. De Bono's address, in its varied approaches to thinking, culminates in the development of a 'thinking identity' for each person. Bawden suggests that students will need to bring new knowledge and new ways of knowing to bear on increasingly difficult problems.

Bawden initially introduces three ways of knowing and learning: *propositional*, *practical* and *experiential*, each validated in different ways. *Experiential* knowledge involves the whole person in its development and constitutes a synthesis of both *propositional* and *practical* knowledge. He then moves on to introduce *inspirational* knowing as a fourth form which provides insights that help make meaning out of what is derived from the other three. It is the form of knowing and learning which addresses what *should*, rather than just what *could*, be done.

Up to this point, Bawden has outlined a position which has similarities to what others present. For example, Power cites the four pillars of learning of the Delors Report (UNESCO 1996): *learning to know, learning to do, learning to live together* and *learning to be*. The first two – *learning to know* and *learning to do* – closely parallel Bawden's concepts of *propositional* knowledge (although the Delors Report's concept is perhaps wider) and *practical* knowledge. *Learning to live together* is present in Bawden's consistent stress on developing knowledge in ways that will improve both oneself and the world, the two being indissolubly linked. His example of the development of a systemic approach to agricultural education at Hawkesbury embodies and values *learning to live together*, but he does not identify it as a way of knowing/learning distinct from others. Instead, it is bound up in them. *Learning to be* relates to Bawden's *inspirational* knowing, especially in its focus on judgement and action, but also specifically encompasses creative imagination and aesthetic forms of knowing.

The views on knowing and learning set out in the Delors Report and Bawden's chapter are threads running throughout Stages 1 and 2 of the project. In Stage I there was the wish by participants for the development of individuals competent in analysing, choosing and judging. They also envisaged the development of a broad knowledge base as well as specialist knowledge – of knowing *that* (*propositional/learning to know*) as well as knowing *how*, including 'competent performance' in the workforce (*practical/learning to do*).

In Oats's exemplars of the two schools, each has a strong sense of community; each encourages students to know themselves and to place their understandings in the context of other views from different cultures; each encourages tolerance; each has a place for *practical learning* as well as *propositional*, for *learning to live togethe*r as well as *learning to be*. Similarly, in Chapter 7, Elizabeth Campbell illustrates the differing forms of knowing and learning involved in developing humane values in schools and in the community.

In his analysis of MEX and MEY, Hill juxtaposes *learning to know* with *learning to do*, arguing the value of both in moral education. Further, as he sets out guidelines for moral education in schools, he embeds its development in other forms of knowing and learning, particularly *learning to live together* and *learning to be*. He concludes by arguing the need for 'bold educational policies which carry the individual from the mere getting of knowledge to the achievement of critical autonomy, and from this to a critical loyalty to humane personal and communal values'.

Bawden, however, is distinctive in deliberately placing the different ways of knowing within a learning system – in taking a systemic approach to the subject, and then arguing that one marvellous human talent lies in being able to know about knowing (*meta-knowing*), and so be able to monitor its effectiveness. Further, humans are able to know about the nature of knowledge (*epistemic-knowing*) and the assumptions they make as they go about 'finding out' in a process that develops over time. It is a powerful and systemic explanation which enables Bawden to accommodate diversity while assisting unity.

Care and Compassion: Concern for People

Stage I of this project included the desire for a 'society that espouses humane interpersonal relationships', including equitable treatment, care, empathy and co-operation. In Stage II (the Launceston Conference), the theme was highlighted in a presentation by Valadian (1999), 'Teaching with Care: Learners Will Care'. She described a society founded on care and compassion for others as one which would provide security and viability for its future, a feeling of purpose for its members, a feeling of being needed in the community. In addition, it would have defined roles for each of its members, and would have environmental issues applying across a wide range of activities.

Power had spoken earlier of the need to include those who are currently excluded. Valadian took up this issue in speaking of how the European educational system, which became established in Australia, neither recognised nor acknowledged that the traditional community had a comprehensive system of education in which the community had full responsibility for both the education of the individual and the collective education of the group. The need to care for others was a prominent feature of that education. She argued that we need to know our traditions so that we can know what to abandon as well as what to hang on to as we move on. We need to think more as human beings, and less as particularised minorities. We need to make more room for the heart, or the essence, of the various traditions from which we come, so that we can know, value and live with ourselves and with each other. She argued the need for a philosophy of education that 'says the most important learning in our life is that which generates and maintains care and compassion for others'. She did not underestimate the task involved in creating a caring and compassionate society, suggesting that it would require a redefinition of values, and changes to the political, legal, economic, social and, especially, education systems of the country.

In Chapter 7, Elizabeth Campbell takes up the theme of care and compassion in the context of educating for a humane society. She sees the role of education as encompassing four major activities: developing 'reciprocal' relationships among teachers, children, parents and communities; removing inhumane elements (such as bullying) from the school; introducing positive humane elements (including respect for people, care and compassion, and equitable treatment); and implementing a curriculum deliberately aimed at establishing humane values.

In advocating the need for sustainable development, Fien argues for basic changes in human attitudes and actions, not only towards the environment, but also towards ourselves and others. This, in turn, involves a shift to acting in accord with such values as empathy with other species, other people and future generations; respect for natural and social limits of growth; support for careful planning in order to minimise threats to nature and the quality of life; and a desire for change in the way most societies conduct their economic and political affairs. His concept of care includes the immediate concerns of individuals from all across the globe.

Global Responsibilities and Perspectives

The report of Stage I of the project refers to a desirable society as being one 'that is conscious of its global responsibilities', including sustainable development, open global relationships, regional alignments and international responsibilities.

Both Fien and Power pick up this thread, and both set their discussion in the context of ongoing global change. Power notes that in the 'changing global village, the rapidity and scope of the transformations underway not only link our fate increasingly with that of others but also, somewhat paradoxically, create greater political and economic uncertainty, larger gaps between nations and greater cultural diversity within them'. He graphically describes a world characterised by 'inequity, poverty, violence, drug abuse and exclusion, as well as new threats to security and social cohesion stemming from the economic and social structural transformations of the information age'. He notes: 'Globalisation and new communication technologies threaten further marginalisation of the poor and minority cultures.' Fien adds to that description a range of global environmental issues such as land degradation and desertification, and the destruction of rainforests. He agrees with Power on global inequalities in standards of living and human well-being, citing the failure of the world to solve trade and transport problems that cause hunger and malnutrition.

Fien sees the environmental crisis as having an ethical dimension, and Hill agrees when he identifies the crisis in which 'our planet is imperilled by pollution, deforestation and extinction of the species' as a 'relatively new moral concern'. It is in this context that Fien speaks of sustainable development as needing to be seen as a holistic concept, 'as the totality of our surroundings and existence which results from the way we use nature and its resources to satisfy our needs and wants'. This means seeing it as a complex web of global elements, realising that 'environmental and development problems cannot be understood without reference to social, economic and political values, and that managing the global crisis will depend upon changes in personal values, lifestyle choice and global patterns of development and trade'.

It is from such a perspective that the UNESCO project on defining global ethics takes its impetus; that the Universal Declaration of Human Rights, including Article 26 on education, gains its contemporary significance; that the World Conference on Education for All was held in 1990, and was followed up six years later in Amman, Jordan. It is in this context that educationists need to aim 'at both global unity and individual and cultural diversity'. Power argues, 'Slowly it is being realised that the recognition of individual and cultural diversity is required by democratic principles of equity, human rights and self-determination', and that slowly 'we are beginning to see cultural diversity as an asset, rather than a liability ...'.

The Weft

In addition to the major threads discussed above, forming the 'warp' of the project, there are many cross-threads forming the 'weft': forms of education; the role of education; the pivotal role

of teachers; teaching; the curriculum; and collaboration to bring
about change at individual, school and system levels. Each, in
various ways, focuses on action. In Stage II of the project, as the
conference developed its themes, as groups became familiar with
working with each other, and as the end of the week-long period
approached with a rush, participants focused more and more on
how to translate the ideas, the visions, into action.

Forms of Education

In Chapter 1, Campbell reminds us that most humans receive
education in three ways: *informally*, as part of their daily lives;
non-formally, occurring outside of schools and organised by many
different public and private agencies; and *formally*, by way of
institutionalised systems graded from pre-school, through primary and secondary, to various forms of post-secondary. He concludes that '*informal* is inescapable; *non-formal* is becoming more
and more frequent, not only in the developing countries but in
developed ones, too, as re-training and lifelong learning become
accepted features; *formal* is common, at least to primary level, in
most parts of the world'.

Despite Campbell's delineation of education in its varied
forms, of which schooling is only one, much of the project has
concentrated on the *formal* mode, particularly at primary and
secondary levels. On occasions, however, the perspective has
broadened to include *non-formal* and *informal* educational opportunities. Almost always, the formal education processes of
schools are set in a wider social context. Fien, for example, focuses on formal education and its role in 'building civil society by
helping students (1) develop criteria for determining what is best
to conserve in their cultural, economic and natural heritage; (2)
discern values and strategies for creating sustainability in their
local communities; and (3) contribute their understanding, with
that of others, to national and global issues'.

Hill starts by focusing on formal education, but, through his
introduction of the voluntary organisations as part of the educational network in our communities, suggests that both non-formal
and informal education can be important contributors to the creation of a better world. Power, too, largely concentrates on formal
education, although in the section on the Delors Report, he notes
the Commission's wider definition, with education being thought
of in a 'more encompassing fashion', and taking 'seriously the

broader social, cultural and moral objectives of education on which our common future depends'.

The Role of Education

What is the role of education in making a better world, in 'Creating Our Common Future', as this book is titled? The role of education in building a better future is regarded by each of the authors as vital, but not as direct, simple or easy.

Part of the difficulty is the necessity for education to be harnessed in a process which not only changes individual learners but also teachers, schools and communities. McMeniman spoke about creating classrooms with students in control of their own learning because teachers had given them that control. Elizabeth Campbell describes graphically the changes in students, schools and communities which must be achieved for a more humane world. Bawden envisages the development of 'critical learning communities'. Fien stresses that the goal is not just individual change but 'working to transform the social conditions of human and non-human life …'. He sees students not only needing practice in envisioning and evaluating alternatives, negotiating and justifying their choices, as well as planning for the future, but also in 'participating in community actions to bring such visions into effect', and so contributing to the 'process of building an informed, concerned and active civil society'.

Power repeatedly stresses that the role of education is 'challenging', but that it must be pursued: 'Our common future will rest on whether we manage to educate ourselves throughout life for richness and diversity in a national and international context.' He argues that '[i]n agreeing to aim at both global unity and individual and cultural diversity, educationists have taken on a much harder task than formerly', when attempts were made to achieve a forced unity through the 'melting pot'.

Two of the authors even suggest that educators must be involved, or risk increasing irrelevance. Bawden throws down the gauntlet by arguing: '[C]ontemporary education is almost universally characterised by inadequate levels of diversity itself. It is, therefore, failing even to understand, let alone encourage, the phenomenon in any other human domain.' He continues, quoting Hutchins's claim that '[c]ivilization can be saved only by a moral, intellectual and spiritual revolution to match the scientific, technological and economic revolution in which we are living. If education can contribute to that then it offers a real hope of salvation to suffering humanity everywhere. If it cannot, or will not ... then it is irrelevant, and its fate is immaterial'.

Fien writes with similar intensity about the role of education in achieving sustainability, also suggesting, through Orr's words, that if educators do not become directly engaged in achieving this goal, then they and education itself become irrelevant: 'Sustainability is about the terms and conditions of human survival.... Those presuming to educate should not stand aloof from the decision about how and whether life will be lived in the twenty-first century. To do so would be to miss the Mount Everest issues on the historical topography of our age, and condemn ourselves to irrelevance.'

Teachers: A Pivotal Role

Power, in concluding his presentation, stresses the pivotal role of teachers. Hill similarly sees the teacher as critical. He argues that while schools and teachers may not be able to do 'the whole job' of moral education, they have responsibility for a 'substantial agenda', which includes informing students of the worlds of value, functioning in a pluralistic society, developing tools of analysis and empathy, and encouraging the 'kinds of interaction that make for a caring and convivial society'.

Several of the contributors emphasise the importance of the learning context reinforcing what is taught. In Chapter 4, The Friends' School is presented as placing a high value on its teachers and on the role models they present to their students. The quality of relationships developed among those in the school community is a vital part of a learner's education. In such a setting, the 'special contribution' of the teacher is to confirm the 'deepest thing' which a student has within her or him. The potential influence of context and educational programme extends to every facet of living and being. Elizabeth Campbell similarly sees congruence of context and learning programme and approach as vital. The programme she proposes for reform centres on changing the context in which learning occurs, as well as the curriculum.

Fien, in presenting teachers as central to the implementation of environmental education and the achievement of sustainability, argues for the constant interaction between classroom and community. He describes the approach he is seeking to have implemented as 'holistic'. Bawden's perspective is also holistic but stems from a different set of premises. In the Hawkesbury case-study, he describes academics serving in three concurrent roles: facilitators of group learning projects; facilitators to individual students; and 'content resource people'. One could imagine teachers in Fien's enquiry-based approach operating in these three modes. Bawden, however, also presents, through the description of the development of the Hawkesbury agricultural programme, an approach which is holistic in terms of its systemic base. He describes the development of a 'learning system':

'... the final realisation was that the whole Faculty and all of the activities in which it engaged, on and off campus, could be seen and valued from a critical learning system perspective. We were, indeed, learning how to be systemic, and how to help others do likewise....'

Teaching

The skills, approach, values and techniques of teachers are seen as central by those making keynote addresses in Stage II as well as the authors of earlier chapters, with their views varying a good deal.

On the one hand, Valadian suggested that the community has a prime role – a rather different emphasis on community than that suggested by the other keynote speakers and authors. McMeniman and de Bono, on the other hand, suggest the impact that 'cyberspace' is having, and could have, on the role of teachers. In some ways, the teacher's role is being redefined to that of leader, co-ordinator and connector, adept at facilitating learning. The implications widen out from the role of teachers to the organisations they work in, suggesting sites other than schools as major learning settings – the home and workplace among them – and also suggesting that learning may occur at times more suited to the learner's needs than the relatively fixed schedule of terms and timetables of present learning organisations.

Elizabeth Campbell sees the teacher's role already as one of orchestrating a disparate array, including educational objectives, students and others, time, space, psychological climates, learning and learning styles, subject matter, knowledge and its organisation. The complex role draws on the capacity, skills and knowledge of teachers as 'members of the community of scholars'.

Bawden sees the academic staff in his case-study as living out the approaches they were teaching. Oats and Hill similarly acknowledge the connection between teaching styles and techniques and the goals of the educational process. McMeniman argues strongly for teachers to be prepared to disclose to learners how they themselves learn and what they themselves are thinking as they learn. Elizabeth Campbell suggests the importance of teacher support for students' learning. Her comparison of the research on competitive and co-operative teaching styles indicates the importance of the latter. Such teaching styles promote respecting the rights and freedoms of others, accepting the will of the majority, respecting those who are relatively powerless (Power's 'excluded'), showing care and compassion for others, and valuing justice for all.

Fien also concentrates on teaching, stressing the integration of teaching with the curriculum and the community within which learning is occurring. He describes the kind of issues to be included in the curriculum, noting that the underlying principles conceive a fair, equal and just future for all – one which is safe and peaceful, as well as ecologically sustainable and which rests on democratic principles. He moves on to detail the sorts of questions that teachers may ask with respect to each of these areas, and the importance of strategic questioning as a way of engaging students in thinking about change. He argues that teaching and learning strategies are the 'most significant determinants of the learning experiences of students'.

Running through all these images of teaching is that of a professional guide, who poses questions, who sets up the essential issues for learning – constantly. It is not a role for the faint-hearted or for those who are not clear about their values or the significance of learning and teaching in the future world.

Curriculum

The Delors Report's proposal for the four pillars of learning – *learning to know, to do, to live together* and *to be* – represents a broadly based re-structuring of the curriculum. The very metaphor chosen – that of 'pillars' – suggests that the four are to be seen as equal and as continuing at least throughout the years of formal compulsory education. In many parts of the world, if such an approach were implemented, the emphasis in curriculum would have to shift from *learning to know* to the other three pillars, with the re-balancing being greater at secondary level than at primary. The result would be a more integrated curriculum, one with less emphasis on *learning to know* – including the Internet, as it is seen as being part of that 'pillar'.

Stage II also focused on other specific aspects of curriculum. Of these, two are selected for comment here: citizenship, and thinking and knowing.

Power argues for an approach to education which will aim at equipping students with 'multiple citizenships', beginning with 'an acceptance of the oneness of the human family and the interconnectedness of all nations, cultures and religions as we address global and regional problems'. He notes that world citizenship does not imply the abandonment of legitimate national and cultural loyalties, but an understanding of, and respect for, the culture and religion of others, which is possible only if one respects one's own cultural identity.

Fien, too, turns to citizenship as a critical aspect arguing that educating for active environmental citizenship necessitates a focus on the way students learn to make judgements about 'when, how and why to work on their own, and with others, to help build sustainability from the local level upwards'. Citizenship is integral to the concept he advances of 'civil competence'.

Stage II also saw presentations on thinking and knowing. De Bono demonstrated different thinking skills including the 'Six Hats', arguing that thinking should be taught as a separate subject. Bawden, too, seemed to support the explicit teaching of different forms of knowing, using agricultural education as an example, but suggesting the various forms of knowing as an approach to the whole curriculum. His approach is holistic, serving to integrate many different kinds of information in building new understandings and insights.

Overall, even when the authors and speakers touch on different aspects of the curriculum, each argues for integration, rather than fragmentation, for inclusivity rather than exclusivity, and for a clear, sustained focus on both what and how the curriculum is able to be learnt and taught.

Collaboration

The significance of collaboration, to enable learners and teachers to achieve their full potentials, has been consistently referred to in the project. Collaboration between teachers and learners runs right through Oats's chapter. McMeniman, in her keynote address, took the point further, arguing the importance of teachers working collaboratively with learners to encourage them to think about their own learning and to become adept at understanding those processes and at using that understanding to further their learning. The importance of collaboration between parents and teachers, and between schools and communities, is also stressed. It is a central theme in Chapter 4. Hill, too, sees the community, especially voluntary agencies, as playing an integral role in moral education. The formal educational agency – the school – must work with the community for the goals of moral education to be achieved effectively. Elizabeth Campbell points to the vital role of families in laying the foundations of education, and thus the importance of parents and teachers working together, especially in the early years of a child's education. McMeniman, like Bawden and Fien, argues for teachers and students to learn together, and with others in their community.

It is Fien and Bawden, however, who suggest the development of communities. Fien argues for joint action between students and local community as basic to learning, since, for him, one of the tasks of education is to develop the skills of 'action competence'. Bawden takes a similar approach, pointing out that, in learning together, the various participants themselves become part of a developing learning community. His approach allows expansion and contraction of learning communities, as well as the development of links between one such group and another. It is that capacity to link together and act co-operatively which is critical to the implementation of the kind of worldwide vision espoused by the project.

Yet many teachers and schools often feel relatively isolated in the settings in which they work. Many are members of large education systems. For the vision to be achieved, there must be mutual collaboration between teachers and those who control the systems, as well as ways for the various systems, both small and large, to collaborate with each other. The goal is not just collaboration within a community, but between communities, regions and countries.

It is Power who speaks directly of the underlying and widespread shift in power on which such changes depend: 'We need to change our concepts and practices of power in schools, the workplace and international politics, from one based on force, self-interest and aggression, to one based on respect for human rights and cultural differences, participation, consensus and non-violent social change.' As he concludes: 'We have the visions and most of the tools needed to realise them: what is needed now is the political will.'

Loose Ends

The group reflection reports in Stage II suggest the open-ended nature of the discussion of the ideas presented by noting further questions to be pursued. These include:

Human Spirit

- How does spirituality relate to values?
- How does one secure a place for the inclusion of the human spirit in schools across the world?
- How does inspirational knowing relate to achieving, to motivating humans to start learning and continue doing so throughout their life cycles as individuals or communities?

Ways of Knowing and Learning

- What is the relationship between thinking and knowing?
- Are there other forms of thinking and knowing?

Care and Compassion: Concern for People

- Could learning environments that successfully foster care and compassion be identified?
- Could examples around the world be shared?

Forms of Education

- How can formal education be more closely interrelated with the non-formal and informal?
- What are the foundations of learning that motivate human beings to continue learning throughout life and in a wide range of changing contexts?

Teaching

- How can teachers who are (1) familiar with a certain culture and certain approaches to thinking, (2) 'locked into a time warp' and (3) used to formal *what is* thinking move to reshape their own thinking and teach more creatively?

Collaboration

- How can one encourage the various educational organisations, as well as relevant regional and national organisations, to collaborate in translating visions into action?
- How can one influence governing bodies (at the levels of schools, systems, regions, nations) to support the directions that UNESCO is suggesting?
- How can the individual educator establish links with initiatives in various parts of the globe?

Action

- How do we translate ideas, values, ways of knowing into action?
- How do we know when the action is effective?

What Next?

The concluding stages of the Launceston conference saw an array of follow-up actions proposed. Some, like the Japanese delegates, had drawn up an action plan before the conclusion of the conference, setting out ways in which they wished to change the education system in line with the vision presented. The Youth Forum, which was an important and innovative feature of Stage II, began setting up a youth network through the use of the Internet, media and conferences aimed at creating awareness of the issues and sharing ideas about education for a better world. A policy developer in a large education system wanted to review that system's value statement in the light of those presented. Others were going to take up the issues of indigenous education, and develop a charter for working with values in their schools and communities. Most indicated they would like to enhance existing links between WEF and UNESCO.

Then the various participants dispersed to different countries, to resume their varying roles as teachers or lecturers, as parents, as policy developers in education ministries, as community members. The question of what follow-up action has been undertaken, or is being undertaken, or is planned, must be left open and largely unanswered at this relatively early date.

We can, however, report briefly on what is happening where we live. The year-long programme has focused on issues arising from the Stage II conference, and particularly the Delors Report. Students from a university have been linked into WEF. Three seminars on Delors have been held. An early childhood programme from Northern Italy which implements the four pillars of Delors has been discussed. Three schools have each adopted one of the pillars from the Delors Report and are working on implementation in their particular setting. Each presented a workshop on ways teachers can implement the Delors Report, and a video on the work is planned for presentation at the 41st International Conference of WEF. One school has joined the Associated Schools Network of UNESCO. There have been a number of workshops – one on 'inspirational learning' earlier this year; another given by one of the Stage II workshop leaders on how we might shape appropriate technology education for students, taking into account environmental considerations.

A start has been made. Questions remain as to how to sustain such an effort; how to ensure its effectiveness in shaping learning as well as teaching at all levels of education; and how to link it effectively with the work of other groups in other countries, and with UNESCO, itself, in an ongoing and sustained endeavour. What are others doing as they seek to translate the vision into action? That may well become clear in South Africa at the 41st International Conference of WEF in April 2001.

References

Bawden, R. 1999. Learning to Lay Down the Path Walking. Address to the 40th International Conference of WEF, Launceston.

Campbell, J., McMeniman, M.M. and Baikaloff, N. 1992. *Visions of a Future Australian Society: Towards an Educational Curriculum for 2000 AD and Beyond*. Ministerial Consultative Council on Curriculum: Brisbane.

Capra, F. 1988. *Uncommon Wisdom*. William Collins: London.

de Bono, E. 1999. You Can Analyse the Past but You Have to Design the Future. Address to the 40th International Conference of WEF, Launceston.

Fien, J. 1999. Reorienting Education for a Sustainable Future. Address to the 40th International Conference of WEF, Launceston.

Hill, B. 1999. Education for Whose Good? Address to the 40th International Conference of WEF, Launceston.

Huebner, D. 1985. Spirituality and knowing. In E. Eisner (ed.). *Teaching and Learning the Ways of Knowing*. 84th Yearbook of the National Society for the Study of Education: Chicago.

McMeniman, M. 1999. Engaging the Educational Vision: Handing Control to the Imaginative and Empathic Learner. Address to the 40th International Conference of WEF, Launceston.

Power, C. 1999. Concept of a Better World in Cross-cultural Perspective. Address to the 40th International Conference of WEF, Launceston.

UNESCO. 1996. *Learning: The Treasure Within* (Delors Report). Report of the International Commission on Education for the 21st Century. UNESCO Publishing: Paris.

————. 1998. *Universal Ethics Project*. UNESCO Publishing: Paris.

Valadian, M. 1999. Teaching with Care: Learners will Care. Address to the 40th International Conference of WEF, Launceston.

INDEX

Oats, William N., 38, 45–46, 48, 50, 52, 54, 56, 58, 60, 107, 120, 143–145, 148, 155, 157

Power, Colin N., 10, 13, 15, 16, 18, 20, 22, 24, 26, 28, 54, 72, 84, 103, 133, 141, 143, 146, 148, 154, 156, 158, 162
Pullenvale Environmental Education Centre, 75

Rio Conference, 21

Strategic Questioning, 136–138, 156

Tbilisi Declaration, 128, 142
The Friends' School, 54, 56–58, 60, 154

UNESCO, *passim*

Valadian, Margaret, 102, 121, 143, 149, 155, 162

WA Values Review Project, 74, 78
WEF, 13, 15, 28, 49, 60, 71–72, 79, 117, 121, 139, 141, 143, 145, 147, 160–162. *See also* World Education Fellowship
Woolman, David, 117, 121
Working with Parents and Community, 104–105, 120
World Education Fellowship, 15, 48. *See also* WEF